Introduction

Welcome to the *New Headway Intermediate Pronunciation Course*!

The questions and answers on these pages are to help you to understand this book, so that you can get the best out of it when you use it.

Who is this book for?

The New Headway Intermediate Pronunciation Course is for intermediate level students who wish to improve their English pronunciation.

How does this book work?

You can use this book (and tape) on their own. The exercises in it will help you to organize your study of pronunciation.

It is also part of the *New Headway English Course* and the topics and language of each unit in this book link with those in the *New Headway Intermediate Student's Book*.

What types of exercise are there?

There are four different types of exercise in this book:

1 **Sounds** These exercises help you to practise all the sounds that we use in English, but some sounds exercises are particularly suitable for speakers of certain languages. The table below is to help you choose the most relevant exercises.

Sounds exercises

Unit	Sounds	All nationalities	Czech	French	German	Greek	Hungarian	Italian	Japanese	Polish	Portuguese	Russian	Spanish	Turkish
Unit 1	The sounds /s/, /z/, or /ɪz/?	✔												
	Consonant clusters with 's'				✔		✔					✔	✔	
Unit 2	The sounds /iː/ and /ɪ/		✔	✔			✔	✔	✔	✔	✔	✔	✔	✔
	The sounds /v/ and /w/		✔	✔			✔		✔	✔		✔		✔
Unit 3	*-ed* forms with /t/, /d/, or /ɪd/	✔												
	The sounds /θ/ and /ð/	✔												
Unit 4	The sounds /j/ and /dʒ/			✔	✔	✔				✔		✔	✔	
	The sounds /k/, /g/, and /w/				✔							✔		
Unit 5	The sound /l/ at the end of words	✔												
	The sounds /ɒ/ and /əʊ/	✔												
Unit 6	The sounds /n/ and /ŋ/		✔		✔			✔		✔		✔		
	The sounds /ʊ/ and /uː/		✔	✔	✔	✔	✔	✔	✔	✔	✔	✔	✔	✔
Unit 7	The sounds /æ/ and /ʌ/		✔		✔			✔	✔	✔		✔	✔	
	The sound /h/		✔		✔			✔	✔	✔		✔		
Unit 8	The sounds /ɔː/ and /əʊ/	✔												
	The sounds /b/ and /v/											✔		
Unit 9	The sound /ɜː/			✔	✔		✔	✔		✔	✔	✔		
Unit 10	The sounds /e/ and /eɪ/	✔												
	The sounds /r/ and /l/								✔					
Unit 11	The sounds /ʃ/ and /tʃ/		✔	✔	✔	✔	✔				✔	✔		
	The sound /aʊ/	✔												
Unit 12	Revises all the sounds and the phonetic symbols that we use in English.	✔												

Intermediate

New Headway

Pronunciation Course

Sarah Cunningham
Bill Bowler

OXFORD
UNIVERSITY PRESS

Contents

The connection between English spelling and pronunciation is often a problem for students of all nationalities. For this reason it is important to know the English sound symbols (phonetic symbols). These symbols help you to learn the pronunciation of new words easily.

You can find a key to the phonetic symbols on the inside of the front cover of this book.

2 **Connected speech** These exercises help you to pronounce words in phrases and sentences correctly.

3 **Intonation and sentence stress** These exercises help you to hear and practise different kinds of intonation and sentence stress patterns.

4 **Word focus** In these exercises you study groups of words where there are problems with sounds and word stress.

What about the tape?

This book comes with one tape. Some exercises have different sections of tape (a, b, c, etc.). The symbol in the exercise shows exactly which part of the tape you listen to.

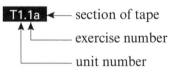

T1.1a ◄── section of tape
└── exercise number
└── unit number

What about the key?

The answers to exercises, and tapescripts which are not in full in the exercises themselves, are in the key at the back of the book.

As in the *New Headway* Student's Book, sometimes we ask you questions to help you work out rules for yourself. The answers to these questions are in the key, too.

The key symbol after an exercise means look at the key. The page number with the key symbol shows you exactly where to look: ⚷── p. 54

What about technical words?

Here is a list of technical words we use in this book. Use a bilingual dictionary to translate them. You can look back at this list while you use the book.

consonant _____

contraction _____

flat _____

formal _____

informal _____

intonation _____

linking _____

phonetic _____

polite _____

pronunciation _____

rude _____

sentence _____

sound _____

spelling _____

stress _____

syllable _____

symbol _____

vowel _____

weak _____

The sounds /s/, /z/, or /ɪz/?
Consonant clusters with *s*
Word stress and the sound /ə/
Weak and strong auxiliaries
Intonation in *Wh-* questions

Sounds

1 The sounds /s/, /z/, or /ɪz/?

1 Three of the nouns below are **always** uncountable. All the others can sometimes be plural. Write an *s* on the end of the nouns that **can** be plural.

government *s*	minute___	game___
computer___	homework___	traffic___
change___	machine___	language___
mistake___	prize___	tourist___
information___	weapon___	

T1.1a Listen to the plural nouns and check your answers.

p. 54

> Notice the different ways that *s* is pronounced at the end of these nouns:
>
> | /s/ | /z/ | /ɪz/ |
> |---|---|---|
> | government<u>s</u> | computer<u>s</u> | chang<u>es</u> |

2 Listen again to the plural nouns and write them in the correct columns in the table below.

/s/	/z/	/ɪz/
governments	*computers*	*changes*

p. 54

3 Complete the rules.

> a If a noun ends with the sounds /s/, /z/, /ʃ/, /tʃ/, /ʒ/, or /dʒ/, the final *s* is pronounced _____.
>
> b If a noun ends with any other voiceless consonant sound (/p/, /t/, /k/, /f/, or /θ/), the final *s* is pronounced _____.
>
> c If a noun ends with any other voiced consonant sound (/b/, /d/, /g/, /v/, /ð/, /l/, /m/, /n/, or /ŋ/) or a vowel sound, the final *s* is pronounced _____.
>
> p. 54

4 Practise saying the plural nouns correctly.

5 The rules above are the same for the third person singular *-s* at the end of verbs in the Present Simple. Can you work out how these verbs are pronounced?

reaches	/ɪz/	hopes	___
watches	___	fixes	___
remembers	___	kisses	___
rises	___	expects	___
tries	___	drives	___
wishes	___	works	___

T1.1b Listen and check your answers. p. 54

2 Consonant clusters with 's'

1 **T1.2a** Listen. All these words have s + consonant at the beginning. How is s pronounced?

space	statue	swimming	states
smile	smoke	spelling	sport
small	slow	Sweden	snow

🔑 p. 54

2 Work with a partner. Put the sentences below into the correct order. There may be more than one possible answer. How many possibilities can you find?

a but / speak / speak / Spanish / Swedish / I / don't / unfortunately / I

b Steve / doesn't / slowly / very / speaks / he / ?

c and / snowing / Scandinavia / it / Switzerland / was / Sunday / Spain / on / in

d sports / started / he / playing / smoking / has / stopped / and

e spare / Stephanie / squash / plays / and / time / in / swimming / her / goes

3 **T1.2b** Listen and compare your answers with those on the tape. Practise saying the sentences as fast as possible. Make sure that you pronounce the words beginning with s correctly.

🔑 p. 54

Word focus

3 Word stress and the sound /ə/

Look at the dictionary entry for the word *average*.
As well as the meaning, you can find the pronunciation of the word, including the stress.

average /ˈævərɪdʒ/ n **1** [C] the result of adding several amounts together and then dividing this total by the number of amounts: *The average of 4, 5,* ● *average*

1 Look at the dictionary entries for the words below. First check the meaning, if necessary, and then mark the stress in the same way.

agriculture /ˈægrɪkʌltʃə(r)/ n [U] the science or practice of cultivating the land and keeping or breeding animals for food; farming: *the Ministry of* agriculture

ancient /ˈeɪnʃənt/ adj **1** belonging to times that are long past: *ancient civilizations ◦ ancient history ◦* ancient

competition /ˌkɒmpəˈtɪʃn/ n **1** [C] an event in which people compete; a contest: *boxing/chess/* competition

medical /ˈmedɪkl/ adj [esp attrib] **1** of the science of medicine; of curing disease: *medical treatment/* medical

politician /ˌpɒləˈtɪʃn/ n a person whose job is concerned with political affairs, esp as an elected member of parliament, etc. politician

population /ˌpɒpjuˈleɪʃn/ n 1 [CGp] (a) the people who live in an area, a city, a country, etc: *control* population

revolution /ˌrevəˈluːʃn/ n **1** [C, U] an attempt to change the system of government, esp by force: *the* revolution

scientific /ˌsaɪənˈtɪfɪk/ adj (a) [attrib] of, used in or involved in science: *a scientific discovery/* scientific

technical /ˈteknɪkl/ adj **1** [usu attrib] of or involving applied and industrial sciences: *a technical* technical

tradition /trəˈdɪʃn/ n (a) [U] the passing of beliefs or customs from one generation to the next: *By* tradition

Many of the unstressed vowel sounds are very weak. In dictionaries these are sometimes marked /ə/, like this:

● *agricult<u>u</u>re* /ˈægrɪkʌltʃ<u>ə</u>(r)/

Sometimes they disappear completely, particularly between certain consonant sounds, like this:

● *competit<u>i</u>on* /kɒmpəˈtɪʃn/

2 **T1.3a** Listen to the words in 1 and <u>underline</u> the weak vowel sounds.

What do you notice about the word stress and the weak vowel sounds?

🔑 p. 54

T1.3b To practise the words, try starting with the stressed syllable, like this:

● *tition*

● *petition*

● *competition*

3 ◀ **T1.3a** Listen again and check your pronunciation of the words from 1.

Connected speech

4 Weak and strong auxiliaries

1 Can you guess which auxiliary verbs go in the gaps below?

a **A** _____ you got any change for this, please?

B No, I _____ , sorry ...

b **A** Oh no – _____ you closed already?

B Yes, Madam, I'm afraid we _____ . We close at 5.30.

c **A** I wonder if you can help me. _____ Bob Mower still work there?

B No, I'm afraid he _____ – he left a long time ago.

d **A** _____ you take credit cards?

B No, sir, I'm afraid we _____ – cheques or cash only.

e **A** You know what – my boss _____ got another pay-rise!

B He _____ ! Not another one!

A He _____ – I don't know why ...

T1.4a Listen and check your answers. 🔑 **p. 54**

2 Listen to the dialogues again and complete the rules.

⚠️

a When positive auxiliary verbs are in full sentences with a main verb, the pronunciation is usually _weak / strong_.

b When auxiliary verbs stand alone without a main verb, the pronunciation is always _weak / strong_.

Remember! Negative auxiliaries do not have a weak pronunciation.

🔑 **p. 54**

T1.4b To practise the weak forms, try starting with a stressed word, like this:

∎   ∎
closed already?

jə ∎   ∎
you closed already?

ə jə ∎   ∎
are you closed already?

3 **T1.4c** Listen to the first part of some more dialogues and tick (✔) the best response below. Try to do the exercise without pausing the tape.

a 1 ☐ Yes, actually, I am.
  2 ☐ Yes, actually, I have.
  3 ☐ Yes, actually, I do.

b 1 ☐ No, he isn't – not any more ...
  2 ☐ No, he doesn't – not any more ...
  3 ☐ No, he didn't – not any more ...

c 1 ☐ I do a bit – why?
  2 ☐ I can a bit – why?
  3 ☐ I am a bit – why?

d 1 ☐ Yes, she is, actually, for about five years.
  2 ☐ Yes, she does, actually, for about five years.
  3 ☐ Yes, she has, actually, for about five years.

e 1 ☐ Really? Do we?
  2 ☐ Really? Are we?
  3 ☐ Really? Have we?

f 1 ☐ No, I'm not, unfortunately ...
  2 ☐ No, I can't, unfortunately ...
  3 ☐ No, I don't, unfortunately ...

g 1 ☐ Oh dear, do they?
  2 ☐ Oh dear, have they?
  3 ☐ Oh dear, are they?

h 1 ☐ Oh no – has he?
  2 ☐ Oh no – is he?
  3 ☐ Oh no – does he? 🔑 **p. 54**

4 Practise the dialogues with a partner, using the full text on page 54. Pay attention to the pronunciation of the auxiliary verbs.

Intonation

5 Intonation in *Wh-* questions

1 **T1.5a** Listen to ten general knowledge questions and find the correct answer in the box below. Pause the tape while you write each answer, but try to listen only once!

Dante	Michael Jackson	4	Bucharest	Texas
15	every 21 days	Sting	every 28 days	1789
Sofia	1848	France	Dallas	the USA
German	Cervantes	Swiss	every 30 days	6
1917	37	Tirana	8	Tolstoy
64	Washington DC	the USSR	Elton John	Austrian

🔑 p. 54

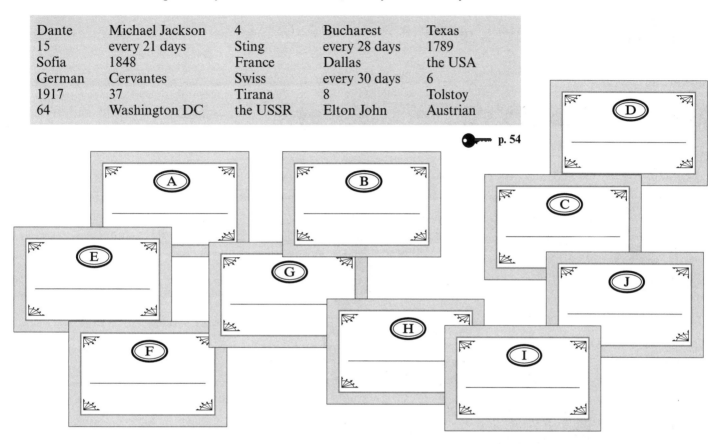

2 All the questions on the tape start with *Wh-* words. Listen again and complete the rule.

⚠️ The intonation of *Wh-* questions normally goes *up / down* at the end.

🔑 p. 55

T1.5b To practise the intonation, try humming the questions first, like this:

MM   mm MM-mm-mm   mm   mm-MM-mm-mm?
What's   the   capital   of   Bulgaria?

Remember to start the question *high* so that it is easier to come down at the end.

3 Use the prompts below to form general knowledge questions.

a Which country / win / 1998 World Cup?
b Who / President of the USA / before Bill Clinton?
c Where / the 1996 Olympic Games?
d What / capital / Chile?
e When / Berlin Wall / come down?
f How many states / the USA?
g Who / write / *Sophie's World*?

T1.5c Listen and check your questions. Practise saying them, paying attention to the intonation.

4 If possible, mingle with the other students in your class to find out any answers that you don't know.

🔑 p. 55

result
result
result

The sounds /i:/ and /ɪ/
The sounds /v/ and /w/
Rising and falling intonation in single words
Contraction of *be* with the Present Continuous
Metric numbers

Sounds

1 The sounds /i:/ and /ɪ/

1 **T2.1a** Listen and circle the words you hear.

a Don't *sleep* / *slip* now!

b Here's some *cheap* / *chip* oil.

c What a nice toy *sheep* / *ship*!

d Have you got any *beans* / *bins*?

e That *peach* / *pitch* is OK.

f Can I have a *leek* / *lick*?

🔑 **p. 55**

Practise making the sounds.

To make the sound /i:/, smile and open your mouth a little.
/i:/ is a long sound. It comes in the words *sleep* and *cheap*.

To make the sound /ɪ/, open your mouth a little more.
/ɪ/ is a short sound. It comes in the words *slip* and *chip*.

---

2 **T2.1b** Listen and repeat these pairs of words.

/i:/	/ɪ/
peach	pitch
sleep	slip
sheep	ship
beans	bins
cheap	chip
leek	lick

3 **T2.1c** All of these words contain either the sound /i:/ or the sound /ɪ/ or both. Listen and mark them *1* (/i:/) or *2* (/ɪ/).

a meets ☐   f children ☐

b television ☐   g week ☐

c eats ☐   h between ☐ ☐

d evening ☐ ☐   i jeans ☐

e office ☐   j England ☐

🔑 **p. 55**

Listen again and practise saying the words correctly.

2 The sounds /v/ and /w/

To make the sound /v/, your top teeth touch your bottom lip.

In English, if we spell a word with the letter *v*, we pronounce it with the sound /v/.

`T2.2a` <u>v</u>ideo   tele<u>v</u>ision   ha<u>v</u>e

To make the sound /w/, your top teeth don't touch your bottom lip. In English, if the letter *w* comes before a vowel, we usually pronounce it /w/.

`T2.2b` <u>w</u>eekend   t<u>w</u>enty   vie<u>w</u>ers

`T2.2c` If you have problems with the sound /w/ at the beginning of a word, try starting with /uː/ like this:
  uuu: → *where*
  uu: → *where*
  u: → *where*

Exceptions

We don't pronounce initial *w* as /w/ in these words:
  who = /huː/   *wrong* = /rɒŋ/
  whole = /həʊl/   *write* = /raɪt/

We also pronounce words like *one*, *once*, and *anyone* with a /w/ sound, although we don't spell them with a *w*.

When *w* comes at the end of a word we don't usually pronounce it as /w/:
  how = /haʊ/   *new* = /njuː/   *saw* = /sɔː/

1 `T2.2d` Listen and write the words from the box in the correct columns in the table below.

| leaves | words | devoted | gives | oneself |
| interview | woman | always | way | believes |

/v/	/w/

🔑 p. 55

Practise saying the words correctly.

2 Practise reading these sentences aloud, paying attention to the pronunciation of *v* and *w*.

We never watch television.
Why would anyone live in a caravan?
Wendy very obviously loves her work.
Have you travelled all over the world?
Twenty of our visitors want wine.
I'm wondering whether to have a shower.

Card A: Sports quiz answers

1 How much did Spanish tennis champion Arantxa Sánchez Vicario earn in 1994?
  c $2,943,665

3 In the 1996 Olympics, what was the men's 200 metres athletics record?
  b 19.66 secs

5 What was the record height for women's hang gliding in 1992?
  a 3,970 m

7 What was the record for cycling speed in 1995?
  c 268.831 km/h

For page 13, Ex. 5

Intonation

3 Intonation in single words

> When we answer questions with *Yes* or *No*,
> our intonation usually goes down.
>
> Sometimes we use single words to ask questions.
> When we do this, our intonation goes up.

1 **T2.3** Listen to these dialogues.
Mark the boxes ↘ where the intonation goes down
(when the speaker is simply answering a question).
Mark the boxes ↗ where the intonation goes up
(when the speaker is asking a question).

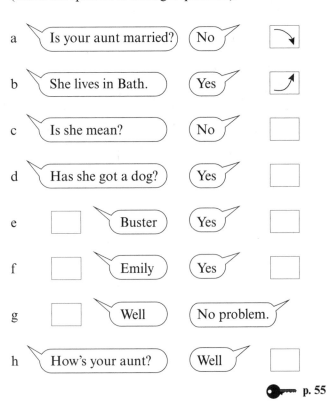

a   Is your aunt married?   No   ↘

b   She lives in Bath.   Yes   ↗

c   Is she mean?   No   ☐

d   Has she got a dog?   Yes   ☐

e   ☐ Buster   Yes   ☐

f   ☐ Emily   Yes   ☐

g   ☐ Well   No problem.

h   How's your aunt?   Well   ☐

🔑 p. 55

For page 13, Ex. 5

Card B: Sports quiz answers

2 How tall is the NBA basketball player Manute Bol?

  a 2.3 m

4 What was the women's record for *skiing* speed
in 1996?

  a 226.7 km/h

6 What was the heaviest catfish caught in 1995?

  b 25.968 kg

8 What was the record for continuously heading a
football in 1995?

  b 7 hrs 17 mins 5 secs

Connected speech

4 *be* with the Present Continuous

1 **T2.4a** Listen to *be* in the contracted form.

  I'*m*
  You'*re*
  He'*s*
  She'*s*
  It'*s*
  We'*re*
  They'*re*

Listen again and repeat.

> ⚠ It can be difficult to hear the auxiliary verb *be* in
> the Present Continuous when people are speaking
> quickly. Because of this, sometimes foreign students
> of English miss out *be*.

2 **T2.4b** Listen to these two students.
Student A says *be*. **Student B** doesn't.

Student A I'm fixing a Rolls-Royce at the moment.
Student B I fixing a Rolls-Royce at the moment. ✗

Student A He's repairing the toilets at the station.
Student B He repairing the toilets at the station. ✗

Can you hear the difference?

3 **T2.4c** Listen to students saying these sentences.
For each sentence, tick (✔) the box if the student
remembers *be* and cross (✗) the box if they forget it.

a ☐ I'm painting a picture of my mother.

b ☐ My company's designing a new opera house.

c ☐ I'm not directing any films at the moment.

d ☐ We're taking *Hamlet* all round Europe.

e ☐ I'm working in Gstaad.

f ☐ They're playing in the World Cup.

🔑 p. 55

4 **T2.4d** Listen to all the sentences pronounced
correctly and repeat them.

5 Metric numbers

1 **T2.5a** Listen to how we pronounce these numbers in English.

Speeds	140 km/h			
Weights	2.6 kg			
Lengths or heights	100 m	1.75 m	10 cm	5 mm
Prices	£1,000,000 $3,995,450	£39.95 $4.50	50p 75¢	
Times	3 hrs 2 hrs 12 mins 2 secs		15 mins 30 secs	

2 **T2.5b** In the table below, column **A** lists the *types* of numbers. Listen to five dialogues and identify the *type* of number you hear in each one. Write the number of the dialogue (1–5) in the correct square in column **B**.

A	B	C
Speeds		
Weights	*1*	
Lengths or heights		
Prices		
Times		

Listen again. Write the number expressions you hear in column **C**.

🔑 p. 55

3 Work in pairs. Take it in turns to read a question and the three possible answers. Find the correct answer on your card while your partner is thinking.

Student A Look at card A on page 11.
Student B Look at card B on page 12.

Sports quiz

1 How much did Spanish tennis champion Arantxa Sánchez Vicario earn in 1994?
   a $5,415,066
   b $3,415,665
   c $2,943,665

2 How tall is the NBA basketball player Manute Bol?
   a 2.3 m
   b 2.25 m
   c 2.2 m

3 In the 1996 Olympics, what was the men's 200 metres athletics record?
   a 19.06 secs   **b** 19.66 secs   **c** 19.96 secs

4 What was the women's record for skiing speed in 1996?
   a 226.7 km/h   **b** 220.5 km/h   **c** 206.6 km/h

5 What was the record height for women's hang-gliding in 1992?
   a 3,970 m
   b 2,970 m
   c 4,970 m

6 What was the heaviest catfish caught in 1995?
   a 23.869 kg
   b 25.968 kg
   c 28.896 kg

7 What was the record for cycling speed in 1995?
   a 831.268 km/h **b** 286.381 km/h **c** 268.831 km/h

8 What was the record for continuously heading a football in 1995?
   a 6 hrs 16 mins 5 secs
   b 7 hrs 17 mins 5 secs
   c 8 hrs 18 mins 5 secs

Who got the most correct answers in the class?

3

-ed forms with /t/, /d/, or /ɪd/
The sounds /θ/ and /ð/
Weak forms and contractions in past tenses
Showing interest through short questions
Transcribing phonetic script: the arts

Sounds

1 -ed forms with /t/, /d/, or /ɪd/

1 **T3.1a** Listen to the sentences only once and tick (✔) the form you hear.

	Present Simple	Past Simple	Not sure
a	☐	☐	☐
b	☐	☐	☐
c	☐	☐	☐
d	☐	☐	☐
e	☐	☐	☐
f	☐	☐	☐

Why is it difficult to hear the difference between the Present Simple and the Past Simple in these sentences?

🔑 **p. 55**

> Notice that the -ed forms are pronounced in three different ways:
>
> | /t/ | /d/ | /ɪd/ |
> |---|---|---|
> | promis<u>ed</u> | agre<u>ed</u> | expect<u>ed</u> |

2 Write these -ed forms in the correct columns in the table below.

created	decided	died	disappeared
suffered	enjoyed	hated	introduced
laughed	mixed	refused	disappointed

/t/	/d/	/ɪd/
promised	*agreed*	*expected*

T3.1b Listen and check your answers. 🔑 p. 55

Listen again and practise saying the words correctly.

3 Complete the following rules.

⚠️
> a If a verb itself ends in a *t* or a *d* sound, the final -ed is pronounced _____.
>
> b If a verb ends in a voiceless consonant sound (/p/, /s/, /k/, /f/, /ʃ/, /tʃ/, or /θ/), the final -ed is pronounced _____.
>
> c If a verb ends in a voiced consonant sound (/b/, /g/, /l/, /z/, /v/, /dʒ/, /ð/, /m/, /n/, or /ŋ/) or a vowel sound, the final -ed is pronounced _____.
>
> 🔑 p. 55

4 **T3.1c** Listen again to the sentences from 1. This time they are all in the Past Simple. Practise saying them, pronouncing the -ed forms correctly.

2 The sounds /θ/ and /ð/

> **T3.2a** Listen to these dates and notice the pronunciation of the *th* sounds.
>
> 25th September 1934   /ð/   /θ/   /θ/
> *The twenty-fifth of September nineteen thirty-four*
>
> 31st December 1943   /ð/ /θ/   /θ/
> *The thirty-first of December nineteen forty-three*
>
> 13th February 1953   /ð/ /θ/   /θ/   /θ/
> *The thirteenth of February nineteen fifty-three*
>
> To make these sounds, your tongue should touch the back of your teeth. If you have difficulty with these sounds, try putting your finger in front of your mouth and touching it with your tongue, like this:
>
>
>
> For the sound /ð/ you use your voice; for the sound /θ/ you don't.
>
> Practise saying the dates above.

1 Can you match these famous people with their dates of birth from the box?

a   Tony Blair _____

b   Brigitte Bardot _____

c   James Dean _____

d   Harrison Ford _____

e   Whoopi Goldberg _____

f   Mao Tse Tung _____

g   Mussolini _____

h   Elvis Presley _____

i   Robert Redford _____

j   Tina Turner _____

k   Mike Tyson _____

l   Vincent Van Gogh _____

> **T3.2b** Listen and check your answers.   p. 55

6th May 1953

29th July 1883

26th December 1893

8th February 1931

28th September 1934

18th August 1937

8th January 1938

26th November 1938

30th June 1966

13th July 1942

30th March 1853

13th November 1949

2 Listen again and stop the tape after each sentence. Practise saying the dates of birth. Say them slowly at first then quicker and quicker. Pay attention to the pronunciation of the *th* sounds.

3 Find out the birthdays (day and month) of the other students in your class. Which two birthdays are closest together?

Or: Work on your own. Write down the dates of birth of some of your family and friends. Practise saying them, paying attention to the *th* sounds.

Connected speech

3 Weak forms and contractions in past tenses

1 Read about Mr and Mrs Bailey. Look at the picture.

> Last month Mr and Mrs Bailey went away for a holiday. They left their teenage children at home. Because of bad weather, they came home early. This is the scene they found when they arrived home.

2 **T3.3a** Listen to some sentences about what Mr and Mrs Bailey saw and decide from the picture whether they are **T** (True) or **F** (False).

a ☐T☐ c ☐ e ☐ g ☐ i ☐
b ☐ d ☐ f ☐ h ☐

🔑 p. 56

Notice the weak forms and contractions used:

Weak forms
Their children had /həd/ invited all their friends round.
Their daughter Emma was /wəz/ dancing on the table.
Some boys were /wə/ playing poker.

Contractions
Emma and Dan obviously hadn't /ˈhædənt/ cleaned the house for days.
The cat wasn't /ˈwɒzənt/ looking very happy.
They weren't /wɜːnt/ listening to any music.

T3.3b Practise starting with the main verb, like this:

	/həd/	
invited ...	had invited ...	Their children had invited all their friends round.
	/wəz/	
dancing ...	was dancing ...	Emma was dancing on the table.
	/wə/	
playing ...	were playing ...	Some boys were playing poker.

---

3 ◀ **T3.3a** Listen to all the sentences again and practise saying them correctly.

4 Write some sentences of your own about the picture, using either the Past Continuous or the Past Perfect. Your sentences can be either true or false. Practise saying them correctly.

5 Work in pairs. Read your sentences to a partner. Your partner should close their book and say from memory whether your sentences are true or false.

Intonation

4 Showing interest through short questions

A   **B**

> I was working in France last summer.   Were you?

> I earned lots of money.   Did you?

1 **T3.4a** Look at these short dialogues between **A** and **B**. Listen and write short questions in the spaces.

a **A** Last summer we hitchhiked to Turkey.

   B *Did you?* _____ ☐

b **A** Yes, and it only took three days.

   B _____ ☐

c **A** We were in Hawaii this time last week.

   B _____ ☐

d **A** Mmm. It was absolutely fantastic.

   B _____ ☐

e **A** John and Vera had a lovely holiday in Corfu.

   B _____ ☐

f **A** Yes, and John took some lovely photographs.

   B _____ ☐

g **A** We spent our holidays in Britain this year.

  B _____ ☐

h **A** Yes, but it was more expensive than going abroad.

  B _____ ☐

 p. 56

2 Listen again. Sometimes **B** sounds interested in what **A** is saying and sometimes she does not. Mark the box *I* if **B** sounds interested and *U* if she sounds uninterested. p. 56

> To show that you are interested and want to hear more, your intonation should start high, go down, and then go up at the end.
>
> **T3.4b** To practise, try exaggerating, like this:
>
> *Were you?*   *Were you?*   *Were you?*
>
> *Did you?*   *Did you?*   *Did you?*
>
> *Was he?*   *Was he?*   *Was he?*

⚠ **Remember!** If your intonation is flat, you will sound bored.

3 **T3.4c** Listen to some people talking about their holidays. Ask short questions. Try to show that you are interested and want to hear more.

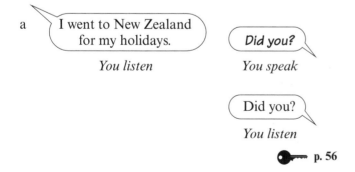

a I went to New Zealand for my holidays.

You listen

Did you?

You speak

Did you?

You listen

 p. 56

5 Transcribing phonetic script: the arts

1 Transcribe the words below to complete the puzzle and read the hidden message. Use a dictionary to check spelling, if necessary.

a /ˈθɪətə/   g /ˈtelɪvɪʒən/
b /dʒæz/   h /ˈdrɔːɪŋ/
c /ˈfɪkʃən/   i /ˈlɪtrətʃə/
d /baɪˈɒɡrəfi/   j /ˈɒprə/
e /ˈpəʊətri/   k /ˈrɒk mjuːzɪk/
f /ˈskʌlptʃə/   l /fəˈtɒɡrəfi/

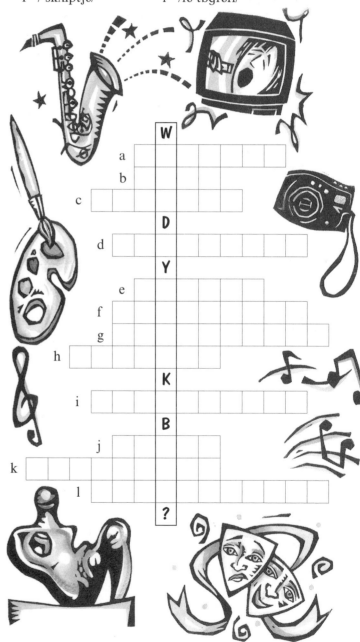

T3.5 Listen and check your answers. p. 56

Listen again and practise saying the words correctly.

The sounds /j/ and /dʒ/
The sounds /k/, /g/, and /w/
Making polite requests
Responding to requests
Modals of obligation

Sounds

1 The sounds /j/ and /dʒ/

1 **T4.1a** Listen to these pairs of words.
Write *1* next to the first word you hear and
2 next to the second word.

a ☐ jet   ☐ yet

b ☐ joke   ☐ yolk

c ☐ juice   ☐ use

d ☐ jaw   ☐ your

Can you hear the difference between the sounds /j/ and
/dʒ/? If not, listen to the pairs of words again.

 p. 56

In English, if we write a word starting with the letter *y*,
we pronounce it with the sound /j/.

T4.1b *yes*   *year*

If you have problems with the soft sound /j/ at the
beginning of a word, try starting with /iː/, like this:

T4.1c iii: → *yes*
       ii: → *yes*
       i: → *yes*

If we pronounce a word with the sound /dʒ/, we write it
with the letter *j* or *g* or the letters *gg* or *dg*.

T4.1d *jeans*   *large*   *suggestion*   *judge*

⚠️ There are many other cases in English where we
pronounce words with /j/ before the sound /uː/:
    use (v) = /juːz/   *universe* = /ˈjuːnɪvɜːs/
    use (n) = /juːs/   *uniform* = /ˈjuːnɪfɔːm/
    Europe = /ˈjʊərəp/

This also happens when there is a consonant before the
sound /uː/:
    cube = /kjuːb/   *menu* = /ˈmenjuː/
    music = /ˈmjuːzik/

Sometimes there are differences between British and
American English:

	GB English	US English
news	= /njuːz/	= /nuːz/
Tuesday	= /ˈtjuːzdeɪ/	= /ˈtuːzdeɪ/

2 ◀ **T4.1a** Listen to the pairs of words in 1 again.
Repeat them, paying attention to the pronunciation of
/j/ and /dʒ/.

3 Work in AB pairs.

Student A Say one of the words in 1.
Student B Point to the word you hear.

Repeat this until Student A has said all the words.
Swap over.

4 **T4.1e** Listen and write the words from the box in the correct columns in the table below.

European	enjoy	younger	imagine
journalist	tune	jacket	geographical
strangers	you	stupid	universal

/j/	/dʒ/

 p. 56

Practise saying the words correctly.

5 **T4.1f** Listen to the sentences below. Underline the /j/ sounds. Remember there may be some exceptional /j/ sounds before the sound /u:/.

a In his youth, Jerry Josephs, the New York jeweller, used to play jazz on a German tuba.

b Julian Jones is jealous of Eunice's Jaguar, but Eunice Jones is jealous of Jason's jacuzzi, and Jason Jones is jealous of Julian's yacht.

c That huge green jaguar is the most beautiful jade statue in this museum.

d Yesterday George Young stupidly damaged Yolanda Jenning's new yellow jeep on a bridge.

Listen again and underline the /dʒ/ sounds like this ∿.

 p. 56

Practise reading the sentences aloud, paying attention to the pronunciation of /j/ and /dʒ/.

2 The sounds /k/, /g/, and /w/

1 **T4.2a** Listen to these words.

a   cot   b   got   c   what

Can you hear the difference?

2 **T4.2b** Listen and circle the word you hear.

a	cot	got	what
b	cot	got	what
c	cot	got	what

d	could	good	wood
e	could	good	wood
f	could	good	wood

g	curl	girl	whirl
h	curl	girl	whirl
i	curl	girl	whirl

 p. 56

You make the sounds /k/ and /g/ at the back of your mouth. You don't use your voice for the sound /k/. You use your voice for the sound /g/.

You make the sound /w/ at the front of your mouth. If you need to practise /w/, turn back to page 11.

◀ **T4.2a** Listen again and practise saying the words in 1.

3 **T4.2c** Listen to different foreign students making requests. Complete the sentences with *Could* or *Would*. If a student uses a /g/ sound by mistake, don't write anything in the gap.

a _____ you tell me the time?

b _____ you lend me a pen?

c _____ you open the window?

d _____ you close the door?

e _____ you lend me 50p?

f _____ you read this for me?

g _____ you carry my bag for me?  **p. 56**

4 Practise saying all the sentences using *Could*, and then again with *Would*. Pay attention to the sound /k/ or /w/ at the beginning of each request.

Intonation and sentence stress

3 Making polite requests

When we ask people to do things, the words we use are very important. Compare the sentences below:

polite

> COULD YOU TURN THE RADIO DOWN?

rude

> TURN THE RADIO DOWN!

But the intonation we use is also very important.

1 **T4.3a** Listen to these two sentences. The words are the same, but **A** sounds polite and **B** sounds rude. Can you hear the difference?

> COULD YOU CLOSE THE DOOR, PLEASE?

P A Could you close the door, please?

R B Could you close the door, please?

2 **T4.3b** Listen to some more sentences. Mark them *P* if they sound polite, and *R* if they sound rude.

a ☐ A Would you mind waiting a moment?
  ☐ B Would you mind waiting a moment?

b ☐ A Do you think you could possibly help me?
  ☐ B Do you think you could possibly help me?

c ☐ A Can you bring the manager here, please?
  ☐ B Can you bring the manager here, please?

d ☐ A Would you mind keeping the noise down?
  ☐ B Would you mind keeping the noise down?

e ☐ A Could you look after Rose a minute?
  ☐ B Could you look after Rose a minute?

 p. 57

To sound polite, start high and go higher on the main stressed word. Your voice should fall a bit and then rise at the end of the sentence, like this:

Could you close the door, please?

Your voice should sound soft, not hard.

Say the requests from 2 politely. Pay attention to your intonation.

4 Responding to requests

When you agree to a request, your intonation should sound polite. To do this, your voice should start high.

T4.4a To practise, try exaggerating, like this:

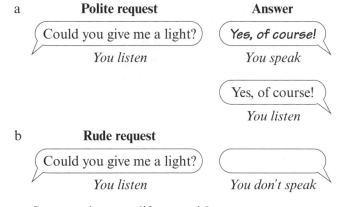

Yes, of course.   *Yes, of course.*   *Yes, of course.*

1 **T4.4b** Listen to these requests.
When the intonation is polite, agree to the request.
When the intonation is rude, say nothing.

a **Polite request**   **Answer**

(Could you give me a light?)   (*Yes, of course!*)
      You listen   *You speak*

                              (Yes, of course!)
                                You listen

b   **Rude request**

(Could you give me a light?)   (   )
      You listen   *You don't speak*

c Can you give me a lift to work?
d Could you pass me the ketchup?
e Could you lend me £10?
f Could you wait for me?

 p. 57

Connected speech

5 Modals of obligation

1 **T4.5a** Listen to these sentences and complete the gaps.

a I _____ email you.

b You _____ tell him about it.

c _____ go home now?

d I _____ be there at three.

e He _____ work very hard.

f I _____ get up at six.   **p. 57**

2 **T4.5b** Remember the pronunciation of the sentences in 1. Read the questions about modals in fast speech. Listen to the answers. Circle the correct answer each time.

a How is *must* pronounced in fast speech?
  1 /mʌst/   2 /məst/

b How is *should* pronounced in fast speech?
  1 /ʃʊd/   2 /ʃəd/

c How is *have to* pronounced in fast speech?
  1 /hæv tuː/   2 /hæftə/

d How is *has to* pronounced in fast speech?
  1 /hæstə/   2 /hæz tuː/

e How is *had to* pronounced in fast speech?
  1 /hæd tuː/   2 /hædtə/   **p. 57**

3 Practise saying the sentences in 1, paying attention to the stress, and the weak forms that you studied in 2.

The sound /l/ at the end of words
The sounds /ɒ/ and /əʊ/
Word linking in fast speech
Emphatic stress
Stress and the sound /ə/ in word families

Sounds

1 The sound /l/ at the end of words

> **T5.1a** Notice the special pronunciation of /l/ in English when it comes at the end of a word or syllable:
>
> I'll ...   I'll help you.
>
> If you have problems with this sound, try adding a short /ʊ/ sound before the /l/ sound, like this:
>
> I' /ʊ/ ll   I' /ʊ/ ll help you.

1 **T5.1b** Freddi is a foreign speaker of English. Listen to these dialogues. Sometimes Freddi gets the /l/ sound right when he says *I'll*, but sometimes he misses it out.

Tick (✔) the box if he pronounces *I'll* correctly.
Cross (✘) the box if he pronounces it incorrectly.

a ☐ **Waiter** Are you ready to order?
Freddi Yes, I'll have a cheeseburger, please.

b ☐ **Ann** Is Clara there, please?
Freddi Just a minute ... I'll go and see ...

c ☐ **Freddi** I'll help you with that!
Ethel Thank you very much, dear, you're very kind!

d ☐ **Alan** We need some more drinks!
Freddi OK, I'll go and get some.

e ☐ **Clerk** Single or return, sir?
Freddi Er ... I'll just have a single, thank you.

🔑 p. 57

2 **T5.1c** Listen to Freddi's lines from the dialogues again. This time he pronounces *I'll* correctly every time. Practise the sentences with *I'll* pronouncing it correctly, like this:

I' /ʊ/ ll ... I' /ʊ/ ll have a cheeseburger.

3 Here are some more words ending in *l*. Practise them in the same way as above.

meal	title	travel	couple
people	petrol	national	cancel

2 The sounds /ɒ/ and /əʊ/

1 **T5.2a** Listen to these two English names. One is a man's name and the other is a woman's name. Can you hear the difference between them?

/ɒ/
John

/əʊ/
Joan

2 **T5.2b** Listen and write the sound that you hear: /ɒ/ or /əʊ/.

a	☐	d	☐	g	☐	j	☐
b	☐	e	☐	h	☐	k	☐
c	☐	f	☐	i	☐	l	☐

🔑 p. 57

Practise making the sounds.

/ɒ/ is a short sound. You make it at the back of the mouth. Your lips should be round.

T5.2c _o_n   sh_o_cked   w_a_nt

/əʊ/ is a diphthong – a long sound made from putting two vowel sounds together. Here the sounds are /ə/ and /ʊ/.

As you make the sound, your lips should close a little, like this:

/ə/ → /ʊ/

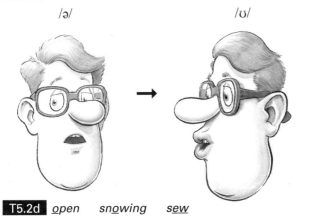

T5.2d _o_pen   sn_ow_ing   s_ew_

3 **T5.2e** Listen to these dialogues and <u>underline</u> all the /ɒ/ sounds.

a John! It's Joan on the phone.
  Oh no! Not Joan!

b It's going to snow.
  Oh ... I won't go home then ...
  No ...?

c OK then! I'm going.
  What? ... oh ... please don't go, Polly!

d He won't show me those holiday photos, you know!
  Why won't he show you them?
  I don't know.

Listen again and <u>underline</u> all the /əʊ/ sounds like this ∿∿.

🔑 p. 57

4 Practise reading the dialogues with a partner. Pay attention to the pronunciation of /ɒ/ and /əʊ/.

3 Word linking in fast speech

1 **T5.3** Listen and complete the dialogue below **without** looking at the box below.

Adam Hello, (a) _____ Adam.

(b) _____ Jess, please?

Paul I'm afraid (c) _____

moment. (d) _____ call you

back as soon as she (e) _____ ?

Adam Mmm OK … if she (f) _____

few minutes but I'm going (g) _____

_____ hour. I'll be

(h) _____ o'clock.

Shall I (i) _____ then?

Paul I think she's (j) _____ on …

Oh, (k) _____ , I think she's

(l) _____ shower now. Jess!

(m) _____ phone!

Jess Thanks, (n) _____ .

Adam! Hello! (o) _____ ?

2 Did you find it difficult to hear the missing words? If so, why do you think this is?

3 Check and correct your answers using the box below to help you.

Notice how words can be linked together when you speak very quickly. You also hear some letters at the end that are usually silent.

Adam Hello, this is Adam. | Can I speak to Jess, please? |

Paul I'm afraid she's in the shower at the moment. | I'll ask if she'll call you back as soon as she gets out, OK? |

Adam Mmm OK | … if she gets out in a few minutes | but I'm going out in a quarter of an hour. | I'll be back at about eight o'clock. | Shall I try again then? |

Paul I think she's going out later on … | Oh, just a minute, | I think she's coming out of the shower now. | Jess! It's Adam on the phone! |

Jess Thanks, I'll answer it upstairs. | Adam! Hello! | How are you …?

4 Listen to the dialogue again. Stop the tape after each section (marked | in the box above) to practise the linking. You may find this easier if you imagine that the linked words are all one long word:

this is Adam → thisizadam

5 Practise the dialogue with a partner, paying attention to the linking so that you can read it quickly and fluently.

4 Emphatic stress

1 **T5.4** Listen to the dialogue between Sally and her grandfather. Unfortunately her grandfather is deaf. He also worries a lot about what Sally does, and who she meets.

Sally I'm going to meet Ann, Grandfather.

Grandfather You're going to meet Sam? Who's Sam?

Sally Not Sam – Ann. We're going to play tennis.

Grandfather You're going to play with Dennis? And who's Dennis?

Sally Not Dennis. Tennis. We're going to play tennis in the park.

Grandfather You're going to play with Dennis and Mark? Who are all these boys you're going to meet?

Sally I'm not going to meet any boys, Grandfather. I'm going to play tennis – in the park – with Ann, a girl … oh, never mind … see you later!

Grandfather Dennis …? Mark …? Sam …? The girl's going mad!

2 Sally and her grandfather stress a lot of words very strongly in the conversation. Listen again and mark the very stressed words like this: Sam.
Why do they stress these particular words? ⚷— p. 57

3 Listen again and read the dialogue with the tape. You can just hum the words, like this:

    mm MM-mm mm MM MM, MM-mm-mm
    I'm   going   to meet Ann, Grandfather

Pay attention to the stress, though.

4 Practise reading the dialogue with a partner, still paying attention to the words that are stressed strongly.

5 Stress and the sound /ə/ in word families

1 **T5.5** Listen and decide whether the words you hear are verbs, nouns, or adjectives. Complete the table below. Notice that there is not always a word for each column.

Verb	Adjective	Noun
arrange	—	*arrangement*

⚷— p. 57

2 Listen again and mark the stress in each word, like this:

    ●   ●
  arrange *arrangement*

Is it always the same syllable that is stressed, or does it change? ⚷— p. 58

3 In Unit 1 you practised weak vowel sounds. This the most common vowel sound in English. There are nineteen words in the table above and they contain twenty-two weak vowel sounds! Can you find them all? Underline them, like this:

  a̲rrange *a̲rrangem̲ent*

Listen again and check your answers. Practise saying the words paying attention to the stress and weak vowel sounds. ⚷— p. 58

The sounds /n/ and /ŋ/
The sounds /ʊ/ and /u:/
Showing degrees of enthusiasm
Disappearing *t* and *d* and word linking with final *w*, *y*, and *r*
International food words

Sounds

1 The sounds /n/ and /ŋ/

1 **T6.1a** Listen and circle the word you hear.

a Look at those *fans / fangs*!

b She *ran / rang* up earlier.

c Were you surprised by the *ban / bang*?

d I'd love a *win / wing*.

e How do you spell '*ton*' / '*tongue*'?

f This is *Ron / wrong*. p. 58

Practise making the sounds.

To make /n/ and /ŋ/, the air comes out through your nose. Your tongue is further back in your mouth when you make /ŋ/. If you have problems making the sound /ŋ/, put your tongue in position to make the sound /k/ and try to say /n/.

⚠ In English, the sound /ŋ/ always comes in the middle or at the end of a syllable or word, never at the beginning.

2 **T6.1b** Listen to these pairs of words and repeat them.

/n/	/ŋ/
fans	fangs
ran	rang
ban	bang
win	wing
ton	tongue
Ron	wrong

In English, the letters *ng* at the end of a word are always pronounced /ŋ/.

When there is another syllable after *ng*, sometimes the *g* is pronounced and sometimes it isn't.

3 Look at the letters *ng* in the words below and cross out the *g* if it is not pronounced.

youngest	sin̶g̶er	ingredients	ringing	young
language	longer	finger	banging	England

T6.1c Listen and check your answers. 🔑 **p. 58**

Listen again and practise saying the words correctly.

2 The sounds /ʊ/ and /u:/

1 **T6.2a** Listen to the example several times to make sure you can hear the difference between the sound /ʊ/ in *football* and the sound /u:/ in *boots*.

Example f<u>oo</u>tball b<u>oo</u>ts

2 **T6.2b** Listen to these phrases. <u>Underline</u> the /ʊ/ sounds.

a good food

b a beautiful cooker

c school uniform

d a wooden pulley

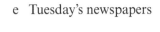

e Tuesday's newspapers

f a souvenir bull

g a cookery book

h a menu for two

⚠️ **Remember** that some words starting with the letter *u* begin with the sound /ju:/:
unify = /ˈjuːnɪfaɪ/

This also happens when there is a consonant before the /u:/ sound:
avenue = /ˈævənjuː/

Sometimes there is a difference between British and American English:

	GB English	US English
new	= /njuː/	= /nuː/
tune	= /tjuːn/	= /tuːn/

Listen again and <u>underline</u> the /u:/ or /ju:/ sounds like this ∿. 🔑 **p. 58**

Practise making the sounds.

To make the sound /ʊ/, your lips should be round. /ʊ/ is a short sound.

To make the sound /u:/, your lips should be very round. /u:/ is a long sound.

3 Practise saying the phrases, paying attention to the /ʊ/, /u:/, and /ju:/ sounds.

Intonation and sentence stress

3 Showing degrees of enthusiasm

> We can show how enthusiastic we are through the words we use.
>
> * It was quite funny. (not very enthusiastic)
> *** It was really funny. (very enthusiastic)
>
> When we speak, we don't always change the **words** we use. We can show how enthusiastic we are through **intonation**.

1 **T6.3** Listen to the first two dialogues below. Make sure you can hear the difference in the degrees of enthusiasm.

Now listen to the other dialogues and mark them
* (not very enthusiastic), or
*** (very enthusiastic).

a **Q** What was the party like?
  A It was interesting. ` * `

b **Q** What was Amsterdam like?
  A It was interesting. ` *** `

c **Q** What was your holiday like?
  A Mmm. It was good. ` `

d **Q** What was your hotel like?
  A Mmm. It was good. ` `

e **Q** What's his younger brother like?
  A Oh, he's nice. ` `

f **Q** What's his father like?
  A Oh, he's nice. ` ` p. 58

Listen again and repeat the answers, paying attention to the intonation and stress.

2 Work in pairs. Practise saying the dialogues aloud. Take turns asking the questions. When your partner answers, listen carefully and try to guess the degree of enthusiasm each time. Is it one star or three stars?

Connected speech

4 Disappearing sounds and word linking

1 **T6.4a** Look at the **bold** letters in the sentences below. Listen and tick (✔) the sentences where you hear the bold letters. Cross (✗) the sentences where you don't hear the bold letters.

a ☐ 1 We're going ou**t**.
  ☐ 2 We're going ou**t** in a minute.
  ☐ 3 We're going ou**t** tonight.

b ☐ 1 I like Chinese foo**d**.
  ☐ 2 I like Chinese foo**d** and Indian food.
  ☐ 3 I like Chinese foo**d** but not Indian food.

c ☐ 1 I'll tell you tomorro**w**.
  ☐ 2 I'll tell you tomorro**w** evening.
  ☐ 3 I'll tell you tomorro**w** night.

d ☐ 1 I saw them yesterda**y**.
  ☐ 2 I saw them yesterda**y** afternoon.
  ☐ 3 I saw them yesterda**y** morning.

e ☐ 1 I'll call back late**r**.
  ☐ 2 I'll call back late**r** on.
  ☐ 3 I'll call back late**r** today. p. 58

2 Complete the rules.

> ⚠
>
> In fast speech:
>
> a We often don't pronounce a final *t* or *d* when it is followed by a *consonant / vowel* sound.
>
> b We often pronounce a final *w*, *y*, or *r* when it is followed by a *consonant / vowel* sound. p. 58

3 **T6.4b** Listen and repeat these sentences. Pay attention to the disappearing letters and linking sounds.

a He likes tennis an̶d̶ skiing.

b My favouri̶t̶e colours‿are yellow‿an̶d̶ green.

c He's very friendly‿an̶d̶ talkative.

d She tol̶d̶ me to carry‿everything!

e How‿are you?

f He promise̶d̶ to men̶d̶ my bike.

g She le̶t̶ them rea̶d̶ for‿a while.

5 International food words

1 Look at the words below. Tick (✔) the ones that are the same or very similar in your language.

a ☐ yoghurt

b ☐ ketchup

c ☐ mayonnaise

d ☐ hamburger

e ☐ chocolate

f ☐ margarine

g ☐ champagne

h ☐ tea

i ☐ oranges

j ☐ pizza

k ☐ sandwich

l ☐ mustard

m ☐ biscuits

n ☐ bananas

Try to guess how the words are pronounced in English.

2 **T6.5** Listen and count how many words you guessed correctly. 🔑 **p. 58**

Listen again and practise saying the words with the correct English pronunciation.

7

The sounds /æ/ and /ʌ/
The sound /h/
The weak forms of *for*
Question tags with falling intonation
Stress in multi-word verbs

Sounds

1 The sounds /æ/ and /ʌ/

1   Write in the Past Simple and past participle of the verbs below.

a   run   _____   _____

b   sing   _____   _____

c   ring   _____   _____

d   swim   _____   _____

e   begin   _____   _____

f   drink   _____   _____

🔑 p. 58

2   **T7.1a** Can you hear the difference between the Past Simple (spelt with *a*) and the past participle (spelt with *u*)?

/æ/   /ʌ/
ran   run

3   **T7.1b** Look back at 1 above. Listen and circle the verb you hear: Past Simple or past participle.

Example (ran)   *run*   🔑 p. 58

Practise making the sounds.

To make the sound /æ/, your mouth should be open, like this: /æ/

T7.1c *apple   match   drank*

To make the sound /ʌ/, your mouth should be less open, like this: /ʌ/

T7.1d *up   much   flood*

---

4   Of course in a sentence the grammar also helps you to identify the Past Simple or past participle. Circle the verb in the correct tense in the the sentences below.

a   ☐   Look! The children (drank)/ *have drunk* everything before they left.

b   ☐   Her boyfriend *rang / has rung* her eight times yesterday.

c   ☐   I'm sorry you can't go into the theatre – the play *already began / has already begun*.

d   ☐   I *just swam / have just swum* a kilometre.

e   ☐   I don't feel very well – I *drank / have drunk* ten whiskies last night.

f   ☐   My legs hurt – I *ran / have run* ten miles yesterday.   🔑 p. 58

5   **T7.1e** Listen to a student reading the sentences aloud. Tick (✔) the box if the verb is pronounced correctly. Cross (✗) the box if it is pronounced incorrectly.

🔑 p. 58

Practise saying the sentences correctly.

2 The sound /h/

1 **T7.2** Listen to the sentences below and <u>underline</u> the /h/ sounds you hear.

  a <u>H</u>elen has cut her own <u>h</u>air again – it's absolutely <u>h</u>orrible.

  b Have you heard about Hanna's horrific adventure in Hamburg?

  c Henry's Uncle Herbert has had another heart attack in hospital.

  d Old Harry hasn't eaten his ham and eggs already, has he?

  e Hazel and Alan have had another unhappy holiday hitch-hiking in Austria and Hungary.

 p. 58

2 There are six words where the letter *h* is not pronounced. Cross out these *h*s, like this ⱨ.

  What sort of words have silent *h*s?
  Why do you think the *h* is silent? p. 58

To make the sound /h/, push a lot of air out of your mouth. The sound is similar to the noise you make when you are out of breath.

/h/

3 Practise saying each of the sentences in 1 five times. Start by saying it very slowly, and then say it faster and faster. Pay attention to the /h/ sounds. Be careful not to put in any extra /h/ sounds.

4 Look at the words below. Seven of them are 'exceptions'. They are not weak forms but the *h* at the beginning of the syllable is not pronounced. Use a dictionary to find the seven words. Check the meaning of any new words.

hole	whole	childhood	honest
how	vehicle	exhibition	heir
hour	behind	rehearse	inherit
who	ghost	dishonest	

Close your book. Can you remember the seven words where *h* is not pronounced? p. 59

Connected speech

3 The weak forms of *for*

> When the word *for* comes in the middle of a phrase or sentence, it is not pronounced /fɔː/, but either /fə/ or /fər/.

1 **T7.3a** Listen to these expressions with *for* and write them in the correct column.

/fə/	/fər/
for ten years	

 p. 59

2 What is the difference between the expressions with /fə/ and those with /fər/?

  Why do you think we pronounce the /r/ in /fər/? p. 59

Practise saying the expressions correctly. With the expressions in the second column, link the /r/ sound onto the beginning of the next word, like this:

  for‿a week or two

3 **T7.3b** Listen and answer the questions on the tape using the prompts below, like this:

  a *fourteen years*

> How long have you known her?

You listen

> *Oh, I've known her for fourteen years.*

You speak

> Oh, I've known her for fourteen years.

You listen

  b *for ages and ages*
  c *for a couple of months*
  d *for four or five days*
  e *twenty-five years*
  f *for a fortnight*

Pay attention to your pronunciation of *for*. p. 59

4 Question tags with falling intonation

1   Steve is applying for the job of chief computer programmer at ABC Computers. Margaret Peters is interviewing him. Listen and complete their dialogue.

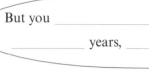 p. 59

You _____ to Manchester University, _____ ?

Yes, _____ .

But you _____ in Canada for _____ years, _____ ?

Yes, I _____ .

2 Listen again to what Margaret says. Do you think she already knows these facts about Steve or not?

p. 59

The questions at the end of the sentences are called **question tags**.

In this dialogue the question tags go **down** at the end because Margaret already knows the answer to the question – she is just using the question tag to **check the information**.

Notice that the sentences are affirmative but the question tags are **negative**.

T7.4b To practise, try exaggerating, like this:

Didn't you?   *Didn't you?*   *Didn't you?*

You went to Manchester University, didn't you?

3 Here are some more things that Margaret says. Complete the sentences with *didn't you?* or *haven't you?*

a You studied computer science at university, _____ ?

b You finished your degree in 1987, _____ ?

c You've worked for Banana Computers since then, _____ ?

d You went to Canada in 1989, _____ ?

e You've also worked in Australia, _____ ?

f You lived in Melbourne, _____ ?

4 T7.4c Listen and practise saying the sentences in 3. Check your answers.

p. 59

Word focus

5 Stress in multi-word verbs

Separable multi-word verbs

1 All the multi-word verbs below can either be separated or not separated. Use the prompts to form the sentence in two different ways, like this:

> Just a minute I'll ~ the light (turn on)
> *Just a minute, I'll <u>turn on</u> the light.*
> *Just a minute, I'll <u>turn</u> the light <u>on</u>.*

a Can you ~ the receiver please (pick up)

b ~ the new words in your dictionaries (look up)

c We had to ~ the meeting because of the terrible weather (put off)

d At bedtime my mother used to ~ wonderful stories for us (make up)

e His parents ~ James and his brothers very strictly (bring up)

2 **T7.5a** Listen and check your answers. Listen to the two types of sentence again. Is the preposition stressed or not in each type? 🔑 p. 59

T7.5b Practise the sentences, paying attention to the stress. If you find this difficult, try humming the pattern first, like this:

```
   □           ■
mm MM mm mm MM
I'll turn on the light.

   □        ■    □
mm MM mm MM MM
I'll turn the light on.
```

⚠ **Remember** to check in a dictionary whether or not multi-word verbs are separable.

Multi-word verbs with two prepositions

3 Look at the exercise below on multi-word verbs with two prepositions. Someone has done the exercise, but unfortunately it is all **wrong**! Rewrite the sentences with the correct multi-word verb. (Sometimes you will need to change the verb forms.)

> **EXERCISE**
>
> a I think Emma's ~~was~~ *run out of* her boyfriend somewhere tonight. ✗
>
> b Do you *fall out with* ~~your~~ your mother-in-law OK? ✗
>
> c We're really *getting on with* your party – it'll be great to see you! ✗
>
> d We've *gone ~~to~~ out with* nice bread – could you get some more when you go to the shops? ✗
>
> e Unfortunately he *looked forward to* his parents last year for some reason – they haven't spoken to each other since then, apparently! ✗

T7.5c Listen and check your answers. 🔑 p. 59

4 Listen again and notice the stress in the multi-word verbs with two prepositions. Tick (✔) the correct rule below:

⚠
a ☐ They are both stressed equally.
b ☐ The first is stressed and the second is weak.
c ☐ The second is stressed and the first is weak.

🔑 p. 59

5 Practise saying the sentences with the correct stress pattern.

The sounds /ɔ:/ and /əʊ/
The sounds /b/ and /v/
Intonation with *really* and *absolutely*
Contractions of *will* and *would*
Adjectives ending in *-ed* and *-ing*

Sounds

1 The sounds /ɔ:/ and /əʊ/

The sound /ɔ:/ is a long vowel.

T8.1a <u>aw</u>ful f<u>a</u>ll m<u>o</u>re

The sound /əʊ/ is a double vowel, or diphthong.
We make it with the sound /ə/ followed by the sound /ʊ/.

T8.1b <u>O</u>K b<u>oat</u> ag<u>o</u>

1 **T8.1c** Listen and tick (✔) the best reply for the words you hear.

a What a big hall!   What a big hole!
  1 ☐ Yes, and the living room's even bigger.
  2 ☐ Yes, I must take it to the shoe repair place.

b Can I have that ball?   Can I have that bowl?
  1 ☐ No, I'm playing tennis with it.
  2 ☐ No, I'm going to put the salad in it.

c Shall I saw that for you?   Shall I sew that for you?
  1 ☐ No, thanks. I like woodwork!
  2 ☐ No, thanks. I like dressmaking!

d I like that boar!   I like that bow!
  1 ☐ I prefer the zebra.
  2 ☐ I'm not very interested in weapons.

e What a lot of noughts!   What a lot of notes!
  1 ☐ Yes. It's too expensive for me, I'm afraid.
  2 ☐ Yes. I'm not sure if I can sing them all properly.

 p. 59

Practise making the sounds.

To make the sound /ɔ:/, you make your lips round. /ɔ:/ is a long sound.

If you need to practise /əʊ/, turn back to page 23.

/ɔ:/

Practise making the sounds.

To make the sound /b/, you put your lips together and push out the air. You use your voice to make /b/. It is a very short sound.

If you need to practise /v/, turn back to page 11.

/b/

2 **T8.1d** Listen and write the words from the box in the correct columns in the table below.

no	four	broken	door	organization	go
law	home	causes	oldest	horse	won't

/ɔ:/	/əʊ/

 p. 59

Practise saying the words correctly.

2 The sounds /b/ and /v/

In English, if we spell a word with the letters *b* or *bb*, we pronounce it with the sound /b/.

T8.2a <u>b</u>ig ho<u>bb</u>ies jo<u>b</u>

In English, if we spell a word with the letter *v*, we pronounce it with the sound /v/.

T8.2b <u>v</u>ery e<u>v</u>ening mo<u>v</u>e

1 **T8.2c** Listen and circle the word you hear.

a Would you like a *bet / vet*?

b I only want the *best / vest*.

c Shall we take a *boat / vote*?

d Hmm, there's something wrong with your *bowels / vowels*.

e There are some *bats / vats* in the cellar.

 p. 59

2 **T8.2d** Listen and repeat these pairs of words.

/b/	/v/
bet	vet
best	vest
boat	vote
bowels	vowels
bats	vats

3 Work with a partner to test each other's pronunciation. You say a word and your partner must point to the word you said.

4 **T8.2e** Practise saying these sentences. First say them slowly, then try saying them faster and faster.

Vera Bathory, the Viennese vampire, bathes every evening in buckets of blood.

A visiting burglar broke Victor Barton's vast Bolivian vase into bits.

Bob Vicks, the village baker, loves Betty Vole, the barmaid at the Bull.

Intonation and sentence stress

3 Intonation with *really* and *absolutely*

> We can use *really* or *absolutely* to make a strong adjective stronger.
>
> **T8.3a** Listen to these dialogues.
>
> **A** What was your holiday like?
> **B** It was really wonderful.
>
> **A** What was the weather like?
> **B** It was absolutely marvellous.

1 Check the pronunciation of the following words in a dictionary. Mark the stress.

hilarious	delicious	fascinating
terrified	exhausted	filthy

 p. 60

2 Try to guess which of the words go into the dialogues below. Don't write the answers.

a **A** Are you tired?
   B I'm absolutely _____ .

b **A** Was the kitchen a bit dirty?
   B It was really _____ .

c **A** Are those sausages tasty?
   B They're absolutely _____ .

d **A** Was that film funny?
   B It was really _____ .

e **A** That book seems interesting.
   B It's absolutely _____ .

f **A** Were you frightened by the ghost?
   B We were really _____ .

T8.3b Listen and write in the words. **p. 60**

> Notice the intonation of *really* or *absolutely* + strong adjective.
>
> **T8.3c** To practise, try exaggerating, like this:
>
> ■↘ ■↘
> *I was really exhausted.*
>
> ■↘ ■↘
> *I was absolutely exhausted.*

3 Work with a partner. Practise reading the dialogues in 2 aloud together. Take it in turns to be **B**. Pay attention to the stress and intonation of *really* or *absolutely* + strong adjective.

Connected speech

4 Contractions of *will* and *would*

1 **T8.4a** Listen to the mini-dialogues.
Write **1** in the box if the answer to the question is in the first conditional and **2** if the answer is in the second conditional.
Listen only once and do not stop the tape.

a (Are you going jogging?)
   ☐ (I (go) if it (stop) raining.)
   _____

b (I think she needs help.)
   ☐ (Well, I (help) her if she (ask) me.)
   _____ _____

c (Can't you work a bit faster?)
   ☐ (I (work) faster if you (pay) me more.)
   _____

d (What's the matter?)
   ☐ (You (be) angry if I (tell) you …)
   _____

e [He's got a terrible cough.]

☐ [Yes. If he (stop) smoking, it (get) better.]

_____ _____

f [Are you going clubbing this evening?]

☐ [If there (be) a football match on TV,
I (stay) at home.]

_____ _____

2 Without listening to the tape, write the two verbs in
the correct form under the speech bubbles, according
to whether the sentence is in the first or second
conditional.

Listen again and check your answers. **p. 60**

3 Can you hear the difference between the contractions
'll and *'d*?

It is important to say the contractions correctly.

If you need to practise the contraction with *will*, turn
back to page 22.

T8.4b Practise the contraction with *would* by starting
with the main verb, like this:

> *help her*
> /ə/ *'d help her*
> I' /ə/ d *help her*
> I'd *help her if she asked me.*

Practise the other sentences in the same way.

---

4 Work with a partner. Read the dialogues.
Pay attention to the pronunciation of the contractions.

Word focus

5 Adjectives ending in -*ed* and -*ing*

It is easy to confuse -*ed* and -*ing* adjectives. When we
talk about **things**, we usually use an -**ing** adjective.
However, when we talk about **people** we can often use
both types of adjective, but **the meaning is different**.

T8.5a Listen to these sentences.

a Your granny's disgusted.

b Your sister's disgusting.

In **a** the meaning is: **disgust** → granny

Granny feels disgust.

In **b** the meaning is: sister → **disgust**

Your sister causes disgust.

---

1 T8.5b Listen and circle the word you hear.

a She's always very *tired* / *tiring*.
b Your uncle was *fascinated* / *fascinating*.
c I felt very *bored* / *boring* at the party.
d Your granny's a very *frightened* / *frightening* woman.
e I'm looking for a boyfriend. Is your brother
interested / *interesting*?
f Your aunt was *amazed* / *amazing* when I told her we
were getting married. **p. 60**

2 Match these replies with the sentences in 1.
1 I'm not sure. I know he likes you a lot.
2 Yes. She offered to organize the whole wedding –
flowers, food, clothes, honeymoon, everything.
3 Yes. As children, we felt really afraid of her.
4 Yes. He's a wonderful person.
5 Wasn't there anyone to talk to then?
6 Yes. She doesn't get enough sleep. **p. 60**

3 Work in pairs. Practise saying the dialogues aloud
together. Take it in turns to start.

9 The sound /ɜː/
Weak forms with present and past modals
Sentence stress with *So do I*, etc.
Adjectives ending in *-al*, *-ful*, *-able/-ible*, and *-ous*

Sounds

1 The sound /ɜː/

1 Look at the dictionary entries for the words below.

<u>ear</u>l	**earl** /ɜːl/ *n* the title of a British nobleman of high rank. See also COUNTESS.
f<u>ur</u>ther	**further**/ˈfɜːðə(r)/ *adv* **1** at or to a greater distance in space or time; more remote; farther: *It's not safe*
p<u>er</u>son	**person** /ˈpɜːsn/ *n* (*pl* **people** /ˈpiːpl/ or, esp in formal use, **persons**) ⇨ note at PEOPLE. **1(a)** a
sh<u>ir</u>t	**shirt** /ʃɜːt/ *n* a piece of clothing made of cotton, etc and worn, esp by men, on the upper part of the
w<u>or</u>d	**word** /wɜːd/ *n* **1(a)** [C] a sound or group of sounds that express a meaning and forms an independent

What do you notice about the pronunciation of the <u>underlined</u> vowel sounds?

🔑 **p. 60**

2 **T9.1a** Listen to these groups of words and circle the one that is not pronounced /ɜː/.

a girl (tired) bird first
b worm worn world work
c adv<u>er</u>tisement univ<u>er</u>sity res<u>er</u>ved west<u>ern</u>
d n<u>ur</u>se b<u>ur</u>y sub<u>ur</u>b dist<u>ur</u>b
e learn earn wear <u>early</u>

🔑 **p. 60**

Listen again and practise saying the words correctly.

3 Read the following dialogue and <u>underline</u> all the syllables which you think are pronounced with an /ɜː/ sound.

A Are all your friends from university working now?
B Nearly. Kirsty's doing research work at Birmingham University and Shirley's gone to work as a nurse somewhere in Burma.
A Really? That's adventurous. What about Pearl?
B Oh, Pearl's a civil servant now. She and Kirk live in a suburb somewhere.
A And how about Dirk?
B Oh, haven't you heard about Dirk? He's working in Turkey as a windsurf instructor! He's learnt Turkish and he's earning a fortune … or so I've heard.

T9.1b Listen and check your answers. 🔑 **p. 60**

Listen again and repeat the dialogue.

4 Practise reading the dialogue with a partner.

Connected speech

2 Weak forms with present and past modals

THE BIGGEST SURPRISE OF MY LIFE

ANGELA MARKHAM, 35, of Leeds, was told five years ago by doctors that she would never have children. But to the delight of Angela and husband Derek (40), six weeks ago she gave birth to a healthy baby boy, Brent. Amazed Angela had not even realized that she was pregnant!

BETH BARLOW, 17, of Newcastle, last week became the country's youngest lottery winner when she collected £2.5 million pounds after buying her first ever lottery ticket. Beth who is studying for A-levels and planning to go to university, had left the ticket in her jeans pocket and forgotten all about it. Luckily for her though, Mum Marion emptied her pockets before washing the jeans and checked the numbers on the ticket. Grateful Beth plans to split her winnings 50–50 with her delighted mum!

1 Read the magazine articles above about Angela Markham and Beth Barlow. What was the biggest surprise of their lives?

2 **T9.2a** Listen to some magazine readers commenting on what happened to Angela and Beth. Mark the boxes below:
A if you think they are talking about Angela,
B if you think they are talking about Beth,
E if you think they might be talking about either of them.

a ☐ _____ believe _____ !
b ☐ _____ big shock _____ !
c ☐ _____ found _____ !
d ☐ _____ very big!
e ☐ _____ dangerous _____ .
f ☐ _____ changing her mind _____
  now _____ !

Complete the gaps. Listen again, if you need to.

🔑 p. 60

> **T9.2b** Notice that *be, have,* and *been* are usually weak after the modal verbs shown below.
> They often link together to sound like one word, with some sounds silent:
>
> /mʌsbɪ/
> mus~~t~~ be ... *it must be hard to believe*
>
> /mʌstəvbɪn/
> must ~~h~~ave been ... *it must have been a big shock*
>
> /kɑːntəvbɪn/
> can't ~~h~~ave been ... *the baby can't have been very big*
>
> /kʊdəvbɪn/
> could ~~h~~ave been ... *it could have been dangerous*
>
> /maɪ(t)bɪ/
> might be ... *she might be changing her mind*
>
> Listen again and practise the modals.

3 ◀ **T9.2a** Practise saying the full sentences from 2, paying attention to the weak forms and linking.

Sentence stress

3 Sentence stress with *So do I*, etc.

1 Zoe and Rob are on holiday abroad. Zoe hears that Rob is English and they start chatting in a cafe. During the conversation the following topics come up.

☐ South London   ☐ Croydon

☐ camping   ☐ sightseeing

☐ the price of accommodation in the city centre

☐ how long they've been on holiday

T9.3a Listen to extracts from their conversation. Tick (✔) the topics where they find they have something in common (something they both do or don't do). Cross (✘) the topics where they find a difference.

🔑 p. 60

2 **T9.3c** You will hear five more statements on the tape. For each sentence, only **one** of the responses below is grammatically possible. Stop the tape after each statement and read out the correct response, paying attention to the stress.

Listen and check your answer in each case.

Really? So does mine!	Neither can I!
Don't worry, I have.	Yes, so do I.
Really? We don't.	

I haven't got any money with me.
You listen

Don't worry, I have.
You speak

Don't worry, I have.
You listen

🔑 p. 61

3 Work in pairs or groups. Think about the list of things below. Then tell your partner(s) about:

- two things you've got
- two things you haven't got
- two things you can do
- two things you can't do
- two things you like
- two things you don't like
- two things you did last weekend
- two things you didn't do last weekend.

Your partner(s) will tell you if it's the same or different for them, using the short responses like the ones above. Pay attention to the stress.

I didn't do any English homework last weekend!

No, neither did I!

Really? I did!

As they discuss similarities and differences, notice which words are stressed in the responses.

First statement	Response (for similarities)
+ I'm from South London, actually.	☐ ■ + Really? So am I.
− We can't afford the city centre.	☐ ■ − Neither* can we.
	Response (for differences)
+ We're staying in a bed and breakfast.	■ ☐ − Oh, we aren't.
− We haven't done much sightseeing.	■ ☐ + Oh, we have.

*This word can be pronounced /ˈnaɪðə(r)/ or /ˈniːðə(r)/.

In this book it is pronounced /ˈnaɪðə(r)/.

T9.3b Practise saying the responses above.

Word focus

4 Adjectives ending in -al, -ful, -able / -ible, and -ous

1 Do you know the meaning of all the adjectives below? Circle the odd one out (according to meaning) in each line. Check any unknown words in your dictionary or with your teacher.

a (careful)   commercial   financial
b cheerful   miserable   sociable
c generous   practical   sensible
d delicious   marvellous   wonderful
e awful   hilarious   terrible

 p. 61

2 Sort the adjectives into the correct columns in the table below.

ending in -al	ending in -able / -ible

ending in -ful	ending in -ous
careful	

Notice that all these **endings** have weak vowel sounds:

  ● /ə/   ● /ə/   ● /ə/   ● /ə/
commercial careful miserable generous

T9.4a Listen and practise the groups of adjectives in your table, pronouncing the endings correctly.

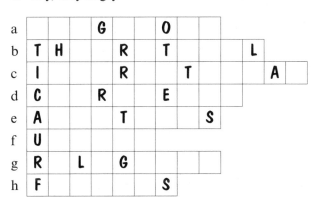 **p. 61**

3 Read the clues. Complete the missing adjectives.

a unsafe
b the opposite of practical
c between different countries
d another word for brave
e someone who wants to be very successful in their career is …
f the opposite of useless
g someone who prays a lot is …
h very, very angry

a			G		O				
b	T	H		R	T		L		
c	I		R		T			A	
d	C		R		E				
e	A		T		S				
f	U								
g	R	L	G						
h	F		S						

T9.4b Listen and check your answers.   **p. 61**

Add the adjectives to the correct columns opposite and practise the pronunciation.

The sounds /e/ and /eɪ/
The sounds /r/ and /l/
Correcting politely
Strong and weak forms of prepositions
Stress in compound nouns

Sounds

1 The sounds /e/ and /eɪ/

1 **T10.1a** Listen to these pairs of words. Write *1* next to the first word you hear and *2* next to the second word.

a ☐ led ☐ laid

b ☐ bet ☐ bait

c ☐ test ☐ taste

d ☐ scent ☐ saint

e ☐ men ☐ mane

f ☐ cell ☐ sale

🔑 p. 61

Practise making the sounds.

To make the sound /e/, you open your lips wide. /e/ is a short sound.

To make the sound /eɪ/, you say the /e/ sound followed by the /ɪ/ sound.

T10.1b Say the two sounds separately. Then say them slowly together. Say them faster until you can say /eɪ/ at normal speed. Remember that a diphthong is a bit longer than a single vowel sound.

Practise saying the words in 1.

2 Look at the words below.
Mark them *1* if they are pronounced with /e/ and *2* if they are pronounced with /eɪ/.

a ☐ cigarette   f ☐ chain
b ☐ they   g ☐ leather
c ☐ death   h ☐ days
d ☐ anyone   i ☐ already
e ☐ newspaper   j ☐ racing

T10.1c Listen and check your answers.

🔑 p. 61

Listen again and practise saying the words.

3 Make up sentences with as many of the words above in them as possible. Practise saying them correctly.

Example
Lots of people had *already* read about the President's *leather* teddy bear in the *newspaper*.

2 The sounds /r/ and /l/

⚠️ In American English, *r* is always pronounced.
In British English, *r* is sometimes pronounced and sometimes not pronounced.

1 **T10.2a** Read and listen to the text below. Notice where *r* is pronounced and where it is **not** pronounced.

> PETER NEWMAN, the Vica**r** of St And**r**ew's Church, **R**epton, in Nottinghamshi**r**e, is celeb**r**ating. He's c**r**ashed his ca**r** a total of five times, and he's turned his instructor's hair g**r**ey. But finally, afte**r** a 17-year course of 632 lessons, he's passed his d**r**iving test.

2 Now circle the correct rules about British English.

⚠️
a *r is / is not* pronounced when it comes before a vowel sound.

b *r is / is not* pronounced when it comes before a consonant sound.

🔑 p. 61

3 **T10.2b** Listen and circle the word you hear.

a That's a nice *rake / lake*.

b They *grow / glow* at night.

c Have you seen my *parrot / palette*?

d She's finished her book about *grammar / glamour*.

e He *corrected / collected* the homework.

🔑 p. 61

Practise making the sounds.

To make the sound /r/, your tongue should be curled back in your mouth.

To make the sound /l/, your tongue should touch the top of your mouth behind your front teeth.

4 Practise saying these sentences correctly. Only pronounce the bold *r*s!

Are you finally celebrating?
A tractor crashed into her car in the lane.
I have problems with the brake and the accelerator.
We're determined to see remote villages.

Intonation and sentence stress

3 Correcting politely with the Present Perfect Continuous

1 **T10.3a** Listen to these short dialogues.
B corrects **A**'s mistakes using stress and intonation.
Mark the main stress in what **B** says like this: ■.

a **A** So you've been collecting coins for 10 years …

 B Well, no, actually. I've been collecting stamps for 10 years.

b **A** So you've been smoking since you were 16 …

 B Well, no, actually. I've been smoking since I was 11.

c **A** So you've been driving for 6 years …

 B Well, no, actually. I've been driving for 6 months.

d **A** So you've been drinking my beer by mistake …

 B Well, no, actually. Pete's been drinking your beer by mistake.

e **A** So you've been writing poems for 20 years …

 B Well, no, actually. I've been writing poems for 30 years.

f **A** So you've been relaxing in Prague since April …

 B Well, no, actually. I've been working in Prague since April.

🔑 p. 61

Look at the intonation. The first phrase starts high, goes higher on *no*, and falls and rises on *actually*. The second phrase rises on the corrected word and falls at the end of the sentence.

Well, no, actually. I've been collecting stamps for 10 years.

To sound polite, your voice should sound soft, not hard.

Listen again and repeat **B**'s part, paying attention to stress and intonation.

---

2 **T10.3b** Listen and use the prompts below.
Correct the information on the tape, paying attention to stress and intonation, like this:

a *Paris*

> So, you've been living in Rome for 10 years.

You listen

> Well, no, actually. I've been living in ■ Paris for 10 years.

You speak

> Well, no, actually. I've been living in ■ Paris for 10 years.

You listen

b *tennis*
c *Friday*
d *housework*
e *repairing*
f *all week*

🔑 p. 61

Connected speech

4 Strong and weak forms of prepositions

1 **T10.4a** Look and listen to the strong and weak forms of these prepositions.

	as	at	for	from	of	to
Strong	/æz/	/æt/	/fɔː/	/frɒm/	/ɒv/	/tuː/
Weak	/əz/	/ət/	/fə/	/frəm/	/əv/	/tə/

Listen again and repeat.

2 **T10.4b** Listen and complete these short dialogues.

a **A** How long are you here ____ ?

 B Only ____ another week ____ the most.

b **C** What did her mother die ____ ?

 D I'm not sure. ____ cancer, I think.

c **E** But where did you get the idea ____ ?

 F ____ my time ____ a tourist in India, actually.

 E And which publisher did you go ____ ?

 F ____ Camford University Press, ____ course.

🔑 p. 61

3 Remember how the strong and weak forms of these words sound. Listen again and mark the boxes *S* when the words are strong and *W* when they are weak.

When are the strong forms used in these dialogues?

 p. 62

4 Listen and repeat the dialogues, paying attention to the strong or weak forms of the prepositions.

5 Work with a partner. Ask and answer the following questions. Pay attention to your pronunciation of strong and weak forms.

● Imagine you have a grant to study. Which university or college would you like to study at?

● Imagine you can change your job. Which company would you like to work for?

● What would you like to work as?

● Imagine you have won an airline competition. Which country in the world would you like to go to?

● Where are your parents from? Where were your grandparents from?

● Do you have any dreams of doing something or buying something in the future? What do you dream of?

Word focus

5 Stress in compound nouns

1 Put one word from the box in each space to make three compound nouns. Use the pictures and a dictionary to help you.

| key | chair | machine | nail | rack | phone |

a washing
    fax _____
    sewing

b _____ box
    card
    book

c arm
    wheel _____
    push

d _____ brush
    file
    varnish

e wine
    roof _____
  luggage

f _____ board
    hole
    ring

 p. 62

2 Which word carries the main stress in each case? Your dictionary will often tell you the stress in compounds, like this:

the dictionary shows the stress here

■ ˈ**washing machine** *n* an electric machine for washing clothes.

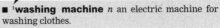 **p. 62**

3 **T10.5** Listen and practise saying the compound words, paying attention to stress.

The sounds /ʃ/ and /tʃ/
The sound /aʊ/
Understanding fast speech
Rising and falling intonation in question tags
Transcribing words about city life

Sounds

1 The sounds /ʃ/ and /tʃ/

1 **T11.1a** Listen and circle the word you hear twice.

a sherry   cherry

b shin   chin

c ships   chips

d wish   witch

e shops   chops

f wash   watch

Listen again and repeat.   🔑 p. 62

Practise making the sounds.

To make these sounds, your tongue should be high up in your mouth. You don't use your voice.

If you have problems with /ʃ/, start with /s/ and move your tongue backwards in your mouth.

T11.1b <u>sh</u>ip   ru<u>sh</u>ing   wa<u>sh</u>

/tʃ/ is the sounds /t/ and /ʃ/ said together.
Say them separately, then try saying them together.

T11.1c <u>ch</u>ip   wat<u>ch</u>ing   ca<u>tch</u>

---

2 Work in pairs. Read the pairs of words in 1 to your partner in groups of three, repeating one of the words twice. Your partner must point to the repeated word.

3 Read the following spelling pronunciation rules and think of five examples of your own.

Words that are pronounced /ʃ/ are usually spelt *sh*.

For example: _____ , _____ , _____ ,

_____ , _____ .

Words that are spelt *ch* or *tch* are usually pronounced /tʃ/.

For example: _____ , _____ , _____ ,

_____ , _____ .

4 **T11.1d** The words below are all exceptions to these sound and spelling rules. Listen and say how the <u>underlined</u> sounds are pronounced.

<u>Ch</u>ristmas   explana<u>t</u>ion   Ru<u>ss</u>ian   ma<u>ch</u>ine

What other words do you know that are exceptions like these? Use a dictionary to check the spelling.

🔑 p. 62

5 ◀ **T11.1a** Look at the tapescript on page 62. Listen to the words from 1 again and repeat, paying attention to the pronunciation of the two different sounds.

6 Check the meaning of any new words in the box below.

portion	cherry cheesecake	kitchen shelf
Czech	checked shorts	chewed
merchant	shining Porsche	purchased
chess	chambermaid	chased

7 **T11.1e** Listen to these tongue-twisters and <u>underline</u> the /ʃ/ sounds.

a Which of Shirley Hatchard's children stole a portion of cherry cheesecake from the kitchen shelf?

b Sheila Charlton's Czech washing machine chewed up Richard Sheridan's checked shorts.

c The rich Turkish sugar merchant purchased a shining Porsche for his Chinese chauffeur to polish.

d Sasha, the Russian chess champion, chased Sharon, the Scottish chambermaid, round the kitchen, so Sharon showed Sasha the door.

Listen again and underline the /tʃ/ sounds like this ⌢⌢⌢.

⚷━ p. 62

8 Practise saying the tongue-twisters five times each. Start by saying them slowly and then say them faster and faster.

2 The sound /aʊ/

1 **T11.2a** In English, many words spelt with *ou* or *ow* are pronounced /aʊ/. Listen to these groups of words and circle the one which is **not** pronounced /aʊ/.

a hour sour four flour
b tower power shower lower
c show now cow how
d shout about route sprout
e town grown brown down

⚷━ p. 62

> The sound /aʊ/ is a diphthong. Say a long /æ/ sound and add a short /ʊ/ sound at the end.

Practise saying the words with /aʊ/ from 1.

2 Work with a partner. Put the sentences below into the correct order. There may be more than one possible answer. How many possibilities can you find?

a lying / this morning / £50 / I found / in town / on the ground / I was / when

b 's going to / now / round / Laura / you / the / house / show

c downstairs / shower room / in the / we caught / mouse / little brown / a / this morning

d and / they've got / you know / town / country / house / house / a / a

e from the / they / to the / tower / ground / cow / of the / lowered / the / window

T11.2b Listen and compare your answers with the tape.

⚷━ p. 62

Practise saying the sentences pronouncing the /aʊ/ sounds correctly.

Stress and connected speech

3 Understanding fast speech

1　**T11.3** You will hear six questions that people might ask you in public places, but they are very fast!

> ⚠ **Remember!** When you hear people speaking English quickly, you don't always need to understand every word as long as you understand the message.

Stop the tape after each question, and think of a possible answer in each case.

2　Listen again and write the number of words you hear in the boxes below (*there's* = two words).

3　Complete the gaps below, replaying the tape as many times as necessary.

a ☐ _____
_____ , please?

b ☐ Excuse me, _____
_____ ?

c ☐ _____
_____ , please?

d ☐ _____
cash machine _____ ?

e ☐ _____
far _____ ?

f ☐ Excuse me, _____
_____ ?

4　Listen again and mark the stressed words like this: ■.

■　　　　■　　　■
Could you tell me what time it is, please?

🔑 p. 62

5　Practise saying the questions as quickly as on the tape. Pay attention to the stressed words.

Stress and intonation

4 Rising and falling intonation in question tags

1　**T11.4a** Listen to two people. Which one is **sure** that he is right? Which one is **unsure**? How do you know?

> Question tags with a rising intonation are 'real' questions, the speaker is not sure of the answer: ↗ ■
>
> *They don't drive on the left in the United States, do they?*
>
> If the intonation falls, the speaker is not asking a question, but just asking the other person to agree: ■ ↘
>
> *They speak French in parts of Canada, don't they?*
>
> **Remember** that the auxiliary verb in the question tag is stressed because it is not with a main verb (see Unit 1).
>
> Listen again and practise the two intonation patterns.

2　Complete the gaps below with the correct question tag.

a 🇺 They don't drive on the left in Australia,
_____ ?

b ☐ They speak Portuguese in Brazil, _____ ?

c ☐ St Petersburg used to be called Leningrad,
_____ ?

d ☐ Austria hasn't got a king or queen, _____ ?

e ☐ Scotland's got its own national football team,
_____ ?

T11.4b Listen and check your answers.

3 Listen again. Mark the box *U* if the speaker sounds unsure and *S* if the speaker sounds sure.

Listen again and repeat. **p. 62**

4 Use the prompts below to make either positive or negative sentences, depending on what you think the correct fact is.

a speak / Italian / Switzerland
b Paraguay / in Africa
c Amsterdam / capital / Netherlands
d have got / King / Spain
e Russian revolution / 1939
f Oregon / west coast of America
g The moon / as big as / Earth
h New York / bigger / Los Angeles
i Greenland / independent country
j seeing a black cat / good luck

Add a question tag to your sentence and read it out to the other students. Show through the intonation of the question tag whether or not you are sure of your facts.

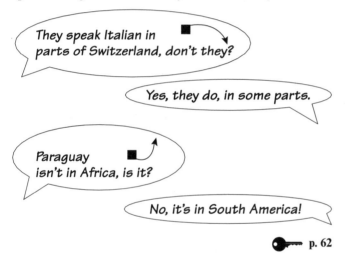

They speak Italian in parts of Switzerland, don't they?

Yes, they do, in some parts.

Paraguay isn't in Africa, is it?

No, it's in South America!

 p. 62

p. 62

Word focus

5 Transcribing words about city life

1 Transcribe the missing words below. (Use the list of phonetic symbols inside the front cover to help you, if necessary.)

a It's usually very /ˈkraʊdɪd/.
b It can be very /ˈnɔɪzi/.
c There's often lots of /ˈnaɪtlaɪf/.
d It can be /ˈləʊnli/.
e There's often a lot of /kraɪm/.
f There's not much /ˌgriːn ˈspeɪs/.
g There's often a lot of /pəˈluːʃn/.
h It's often very /ˈlaɪvli/.
i There are lots of /ˈrestrɒnts/, /ʃɒps/, and /ˈθɪətəz/.
j It's usually /ˈbɪzi/.
k There's lots of /vəˈraɪəti/.
l It's not very /ˈpiːsfl/.

T11.5a Listen and check your answers. **p. 63**

Practise the pronunciation of any words you find difficult.

2 What do **you** think about city life? Make notes from the phrases above in the correct column for you.

Advantages of city life	Disadvantages of city life	Not sure

3 **T11.5b** Listen to three people talking about where they live. Which of the aspects of city life above are they describing?

 p. 63

Vowel and diphthong sounds
Consonant sounds
Showing disbelief
Revision of contractions, linking, and weak forms
Words with silent letters

Sounds

1 Vowel and diphthong sounds

1 Tick (✔) the correct long vowel symbol for each word.

	/iː/	/ɑː/	/ɔː/	/uː/	/ɜː/
a working					
b week					
c moon					
d part					
e talk					

Check your answers. p. 63

T12.1a Listen and repeat the words and the symbols.

2 Look at the words on the left and circle the correct short vowel symbol on the right.

a	son	/ɒ/	/ʌ/	/ʊ/
b	police	/ɒ/	/ʌ/	/ə/
c	dog	/ɒ/	/ʌ/	/ʊ/
d	black	/e/	/æ/	/ə/
e	good	/ʊ/	/ʌ/	/ə/
f	business	/ʌ/	/ʊ/	/ɪ/
g	rest	/e/	/ə/	/æ/

Check your answers. p. 63

T12.1b Listen and repeat the words and the symbols.

3 Circle the correct example word for each double vowel or diphthong symbol.

a	/ʊə/*	tour	moan	south
b	/eɪ/	away	night	die
c	/ɔɪ/	out	bone	enjoy
d	/aɪ/	chair	sky	day
e	/aʊ/	ocean	moan	now
f	/əʊ/	now	telephone	south
g	/ɪə/	fire	here	chair
h	/eə/	near	fire	wear

*This sound is quite rare. People often use /ɔː/ instead.

T12.1c Listen and check your answers. p. 63

Listen again and repeat the symbols and the words.

2 Consonant sounds

1 Match each voiceless consonant symbol with an example word.

a	/p/	1	calm
b	/t/	2	child
c	/k/	3	poor
d	/tʃ/	4	photo
e	/f/	5	tea
f	/θ/	6	sure
g	/s/	7	house
h	/ʃ/	8	think
i	/h/	9	cinema

T12.2a Listen and check your answers. p. 63

Listen again and repeat the symbols and the words.

2 Write a word from the box next to each voiced consonant symbol.

pleasure	door	strange	good	mother
man	ring	light	visitor	boy
closed	nose	friend	well	young

a /b/ _____   i /m/ _____

b /d/ _____   j /n/ _____

c /g/ _____   k /ŋ/ _____

d /dʒ/ _____   l /l/ _____

e /v/ _____   m /r/ _____

f /ð/ _____   n /w/ _____

g /z/ _____   o /j/ _____

h /ʒ/ _____

T12.2b Listen and check your answers. 🔑 p. 63

Listen again and repeat the symbols and the words.

Intonation and sentence stress

3 Showing disbelief

1 **T12.3a** Listen to the following dialogues. Who does not believe what Elaine said – speaker **B** or **D**? How does the stress and intonation show this?

A Where's Elaine today?
B She said she had a headache.

C Where's Elaine today?
D She said she had a headache.

🔑 p. 63

Notice the stress and intonation. To show disbelief when reporting speech, there is a special stress on *said* and the intonation goes down, like this:

She said she had a headache.

The intonation in an ordinary reported speech sentence is like this:

She said she had a headache.

Listen again and repeat the replies, paying attention to the intonation.

---

2 **T12.3b** Listen to the following dialogues. Cross (✗) **B**'s reply when you think he does not believe what he is reporting.

a **A** What did Ben think of the film?
   B He said he loved it. ☐

b **A** Why didn't Carol come to the club?
   B She said she was ill. ☒

c **A** Where did Derek get all that money?
   B He said his aunt had given it to him. ☐

d **A** How's Emma's diet going?
   B She said she'd lost five kilos. ☐

e **A** What's Fiona doing these days?
   B She said she was working as a waitress. ☐

f **A** Will Gemma be at the party?
   B She said she'd go along later. ☐

🔑 p. 63

3 Look at these six things that people in an imaginary English class have told you recently. Tick (✔) the three that you believe and cross (✗) the three that you do not believe.

☐ Pilar said she loved grammar.

☐ Hans said he had a cold last Friday.

☐ Luis said he never made vocabulary mistakes.

☐ Juliette said she didn't have any homework yesterday.

☐ Margit said she hated listening exercises.

☐ Hisashi said he always did well in exams.

Tell your partner about these things. Make it clear from your intonation if you believe what you were told. Your partner should reply appropriately, like this:

You *Pilar said she loved grammar.*

Your partner *Did you believe her?*

You *Yes.*

or

You *Hans said he had a cold last Friday.*

Your partner *Didn't you believe him?*

You *No.*

4 Contractions, linking, and weak forms

1 Rewrite these sentences with contractions.

a I do not like funerals.

_____

b I have been to three christenings this year.

_____

_____

c She is not married.

_____

d He is wearing one striped sock and one checked sock.

_____

_____

e I cannot wait!

_____

f They are eating sandwiches.

_____

T12.4a Listen and check your answers. ⬤━ p. 63

Listen again and repeat the sentences.

2 **T12.4b** Listen and repeat these sentences with linking.

a Not at all.
b That's how it's always been.
c There's all the food.
d Isn't it a pity Ian's wearing odd socks?
e Was ever a bride so pretty?

3 **T12.4c** Listen to these sentences.
Tick (✔) the box if you hear the **bold** *t* or *d*.
Cross (✘) the box if you don't hear it.

a ☐ They came from far and near.
b ☐ Doesn't Isabel look sweet?
c ☐ He's the best man.
d ☐ Find it in the picture.
e ☐ Aunt Beryl!
f ☐ They drank wine and pints of beer.
g ☐ I can't understand.

Look at the sentences you ticked.
Mark the linking like this:

b Doesn't Isabel look sweet? ⬤━ p. 63

Listen again and repeat the sentences with linking and with disappearing *t* and *d* where necessary.

4 `T12.4d` Listen to the poem. What do you notice about the underlined words?

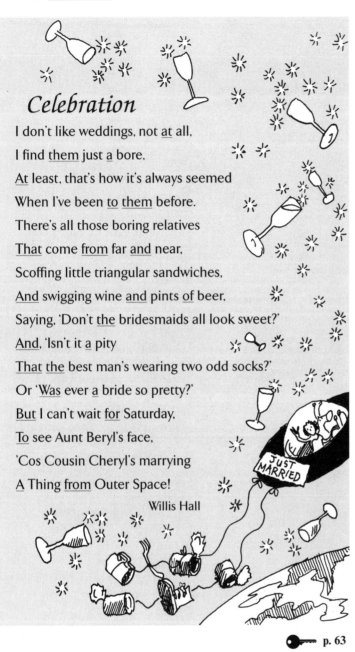

Celebration

I don't like weddings, not <u>at</u> all,
I find <u>them</u> just <u>a</u> bore.
<u>At</u> least, that's how it's always seemed
When I've been <u>to them</u> before.
There's all those boring relatives
<u>That</u> come <u>from</u> far <u>and</u> near,
Scoffing little triangular sandwiches,
<u>And</u> swigging wine <u>and</u> pints <u>of</u> beer,
Saying, 'Don't <u>the</u> bridesmaids all look sweet?'
<u>And</u>, 'Isn't it <u>a</u> pity
<u>That the</u> best man's wearing two odd socks?'
Or '<u>Was</u> ever <u>a</u> bride so pretty?'
<u>But</u> I can't wait <u>for</u> Saturday,
<u>To</u> see Aunt Beryl's face,
'Cos Cousin Cheryl's marrying
<u>A</u> Thing <u>from</u> Outer Space!

Willis Hall

🔑 **p. 63**

5 Listen again. Practise saying the poem with the tape. Pay attention to your pronunciation of contractions, linking, disappearing *t* and *d*, and weak forms.

---

5 Words with silent letters

1 `T12.5a` Listen and cross out the silent letters in these words.

a si~~g~~n   e marriage
b wreath   f guidance
c bouquet   g neighbours
d knocked   h exhausted

🔑 **p. 63**

2 `T12.5b` Listen to some students.
Tick (✔) the sentence if the underlined word is pronounced correctly.
Cross (✘) the sentence if it is pronounced incorrectly.

a ☐ <u>Sign</u> here, please!
b ☐ She laid a <u>wreath</u> on the grave.
c ☐ The bride held a beautiful <u>bouquet</u>.
d ☐ Someone <u>knocked</u> at the door.
e ☐ Their <u>marriage</u> lasted 40 years.
f ☐ I'd like some <u>guidance</u>, please.
g ☐ Our <u>neighbours</u> are very nice.
h ☐ I'm feeling <u>exhausted</u>.

🔑 **p. 63**

`T12.5c` Listen and repeat the sentences with the correct pronunciation.

Key

Unit 1

1 The sounds /s/, /z/, or /ɪz/?

1 **T1.1a**
governments
computers
changes
mistakes
minutes
machines
prizes
weapons
games
languages
tourists

2 /s/
governments
mistakes
minutes
tourists

/z/
computers
machines
weapons
games

/ɪz/
changes
prizes
languages

3 a /ɪz/   b /s/   c /z/

5 reaches   /ɪz/
watches   /ɪz/
remembers   /z/
rises   /ɪz/
tries   /z/
wishes   /ɪz/
hopes   /s/
fixes   /ɪz/
kisses   /ɪz/
expects   /s/
drives   /z/
works   /s/

2 Consonant clusters with 's'

1 The *s* at the beginning of words (except *sh*-) is always pronounced /s/ not /z/.

3 **T1.2b**
a I speak Spanish but unfortunately I don't speak Swedish.
b Steve speaks very slowly, doesn't he?
c It was snowing in Scandinavia, Switzerland, and Spain on Sunday.
d He started playing sport and has stopped smoking.
e Stephanie plays squash and goes swimming in her spare time.

3 Word stress and the sound /ə/

2 ●
agricul<u>tu</u>re
●
an<u>cie</u>nt
       ●
compe<u>ti</u>tion
     ●
med<u>ic</u>al
     ●
poli<u>cia</u>n
       ●
popula<u>ti</u>on
      ●
rev<u>o</u>lution
       ●
sci<u>e</u>ntific
●
techn<u>ic</u>al
      ●
tra<u>di</u>tion

Syllables with the weak vowel sound /ə/ are never stressed.

4 Weak and strong auxiliaries

1 **T1.4a**
a **A** Have you got any change for this, please?
   B No, I haven't, sorry ...
b **A** Oh no – are you closed already?
   B Yes, Madam, I'm afraid we are. We close at 5.30.
c **A** I wonder if you can help me. Does Bob Mower still work there?
   B No, I'm afraid he doesn't – he left a long time ago.
d **A** Do you take credit cards?
   B No, sir, I'm afraid we don't – cheques or cash only.
e **A** You know what – my boss has got another pay-rise!
   B He hasn't! Not another one!
   A He has – I don't know why ...

2 a weak
   b strong

3 a 3   e 3
   b 2   f 2
   c 2   g 3
   d 3   h 1

4 **T1.4c** (The correct responses are shown in brackets.)
a Do you enjoy cooking?
   (Yes, actually, I do.)
b Does your brother still live at home with your parents?
   (No, he doesn't – not any more ...)
c Can you understand any German?
   (I can a bit – why?)
d Has your teacher been at this school for very long?
   (Yes, she has actually, for about five years.)
e We've got a 200-word composition for homework tonight!
   (Really? Have we?)
f Can you write English as well as you speak it?
   (No, I can't, unfortunately ...)
g Unfortunately, both of her parents are dead.
   (Oh dear, are they?)
h Jim can't come tonight – he's got a really bad cold again.
   Oh no – has he?

5 Intonation in *Wh*- questions

1 a Sofia   f 1789
   b Austrian   g Elton John
   c the USSR   h 37
   d Dallas   i every 28 days
   e Cervantes   j 6

T1.5a
a What's the capital of Bulgaria?
b What nationality was Mozart?
c Which country sent the first man into space?
d Where did President Kennedy die?
e Who wrote *Don Quixote*?

f When did the French Revolution start?

g Who sang 'Candle in the Wind'?

h How many plays did Shakespeare write?

i How often is there a full moon?

j How many wives did the English King Henry VIII have?

2 down

4 **T1.5c** (The correct answers are shown in brackets.)

a Which country won the 1998 World Cup?
(France.)

b Who was President of the USA before Bill Clinton?
(George Bush.)

c Where were the 1996 Olympic Games?
(Atlanta, USA.)

d What's the capital of Chile?
(Santiago.)

e When did the Berlin Wall come down?
(1989.)

f How many states are there in the USA?
(50.)

g Who wrote *Sophie's World*?
(Jostein Gaarder.)

Unit 2

1 The sounds /iː/ and /ɪ/

1 **T2.1a**

a Don't *sleep* now!

b Here's some *cheap* oil.

c What a nice toy *ship*!

d Have you got any *bins*?

e That *peach* is OK.

f Can I have a *lick*?

3 a *1*   f *2*
b *2*   g *1*
c *1*   h *2 ... 1*
d *1 ... 2*   i *1*
e *2*   j *2*

2 The sounds /v/ and /w/

1
/v/	/w/
leaves	words
interview	woman
devoted	always
gives	way
believes	oneself

3 Intonation in single words

1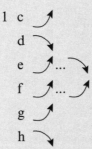
c ↗
d ↘
e ↗ ... ↘
f ↗ ... ↗
g ↗
h ↘

4 *be* with the Present Continuous

3 a ✔   d ✔
b ✘   e ✔
c ✘   f ✘

5 Metric numbers

2
A	B	C
Speeds	5	200 km/h
Weights	1	¼ kg
Lengths or heights	3	4 m 60 (cm)
Prices	2	$75
Times	4	11½ hours

T2.5b

1 A Can I have a quarter of a kilo of those nuts, please?
B Certainly.

2 A How much is that?
B That'll be seventy-five dollars, sir.

3 A How long is the hall where you want this carpet?
B Let me see. It's four metres sixty from the front door to the lounge door.

4 A We were waiting at the airport for eleven and a half hours.
B No!

5 A It was travelling at two hundred kilometres an hour.
B Really?

Unit 3

1 *-ed* forms with /t/, /d/, or /ɪd/

1 a Past Simple
b Present Simple
c Past Simple
d Present Simple
e Past Simple
f Present Simple

It is difficult to hear the /t/ or /d/ sound before another consonant.

T3.1a

a They promised not to be late!

b They always laugh at me.

c We all agreed with you.

d I hate the long cold winters.

e We expected to arrive at about ten.

f They never remember my birthday.

2 **T3.1b**

/t/
laughed
mixed
introduced

/d/
suffered
enjoyed
died
refused
disappeared

/ɪd/
created
decided
hated
disappointed

3 a /ɪd/   b /t/   c /d/

2 The sounds /θ/ and /ð/

1 **T3.2b**

a Tony Blair was born on 6th May 1953.

b Brigitte Bardot was born on 28th September 1934.

c James Dean was born on 8th February 1931.

d Harrison Ford was born on 13th July 1942.

e Whoopi Goldberg was born on 13th November 1949.

f Mao Tse Tung was born on 26th December 1893.

g Mussolini was born on 29th July 1883.

h Elvis Presley was born on 8th January 1938.

i Robert Redford was born on 18th August 1937.

j Tina Turner was born on 26th November 1938.

k Mike Tyson was born on 30th June 1966.

l Vincent Van Gogh was born on 30th March 1853.

3 Weak forms and contractions in past tenses

1 a *T*   d *T*   g *F*
  b *T*   e *F*   h *F*
  c *T*   f *T*   i *T*

T3.3a

a Their children had invited all their friends round.

b Their daughter Emma was dancing on the table.

c One of her friends was phoning her boyfriend in Australia.

d The cat wasn't looking very happy.

e Their son Dan was drinking their best brandy.

f Some boys were playing poker.

g Some of their friends were watching videos.

h They weren't listening to any music.

i Emma and Dan obviously hadn't cleaned the house for days.

4 Showing interest through short questions

1 **T3.4a**

a A Last summer we hitchhiked to Turkey.
  B Did you?

b A Yes, and it only took three days.
  B Did it?

c A We were in Hawaii this time last week.
  B Were you?

d A Mmm. It was absolutely fantastic.
  B Was it?

e A John and Vera had a lovely holiday in Corfu.
  B Did they?

f A Yes, and John took some lovely photographs.
  B Did he?

g A We spent our holidays in Britain this year.
  B Did you?

h A Yes, but it was more expensive than going abroad.
  B Was it?

2 a *I*   d *I*   g *I*
  b *I*   e *U*   h *I*
  c *I*   f *U*

3 **T3.4c**

a A I went to New Zealand for my holidays.
  B Did you?

b A My son went to the Cannes film festival last year.
  B Did he?

c A When we were in Greece the temperature was over 40°.
  B Was it?

d A We were in Rio for the carnival last year.
  B Were you?

e A My husband and I met on holiday in Spain.
  B Did you?

f A Some friends of mine drove all the way to Istanbul.
  B Did they?

5 Transcribing phonetic script: the arts

1 **T3.5**

a theatre   g television
b jazz   h drawing
c fiction   i literature
d biography   j opera
e poetry   k rock music
f sculpture   l photography

The hidden message is:
What do you like best?

Unit 4

1 The sounds /j/ and /dʒ/

1 a 1 ... 2
  b 2 ... 1
  c 2 ... 1
  d 1 ... 2

T4.1a

a jet ... yet
b yolk ... joke
c use ... juice
d jaw ... your

4 /j/   /dʒ/
   European   journalist
   tune   strangers
   you   enjoy
   younger   jacket
   stupid   imagine
   universal   geographical

5 **T4.1f**

a In his youth, Jerry Josephs, the New York jeweller, used to play jazz on a German tuba.

b Julian Jones is jealous of Eunice's Jaguar, but Eunice Jones is jealous of Jason's jacuzzi, and Jason Jones is jealous of Julian's yacht.

c That huge green jaguar is the most beautiful jade statue in this museum.

d Yesterday George Young stupidly damaged Yolanda Jenning's new yellow jeep on a bridge.

2 The sounds /k/, /g/, and /w/

2 **T4.2b**

a cot   d could   g whirl
b got   e wood   h whirl
c got   f could   i girl

3 a Could   e —
  b Would   f Could
  c —   g Could
  d Would

T4.2c

a Could you tell me the time?
b Would you lend me a pen?
c /gʊd/ you open the window?
d Would you close the door?
e /gwʊd/ you lend me 50p?
f Could you read this for me?
g Could you carry my bag for me?

3 Making polite requests

2 a A R   d A R
    B P   B P
  b A R   e A P
    B P   B R
  c A P
    B R

4 Responding to requests

1 **T4.4b**

a A Could you give me a light?
  B Yes, of course!
b A Could you give me a light?
  ...
c A Can you give me a lift to work?
  B Yes, of course!
d A Could you pass me the ketchup?
  ...
e A Could you lend me £10?
  B Yes, of course!
f A Could you wait for me?
  ...

5 Modals of obligation

1 **T4.5a**

a I must email you.
b You should tell him about it.
c Do you have to go home now?
d I have to be there at three.
e He has to work very hard.
f I had to get up at six.

2 a 2 /məst/
  b 2 /ʃəd/
  c 2 /hæftə/
  d 1 /hæstə/
  e 2 /hædtə/

Unit 5

1 The sound /l/ at the end of words

1 a ✗ b ✔ c ✔ d ✗ e ✗

2 The sounds /ɒ/ and /əʊ/

2 a /ɒ/   g /əʊ/
  b /ɒ/   h /əʊ/
  c /əʊ/   i /ɒ/
  d /ɒ/   j /əʊ/
  e /ɒ/   k /əʊ/
  f /əʊ/   l /ɒ/

T5.2b

a not   g won't
b got   h cola
c goat   i pop
d shone   j note
e shop   k shown
f hope   l want

3 a John! It's Joan on the phone.
    Oh no! Not Joan!

  b It's going to snow.
    Oh ... I won't go home then ...
    No ...?

  c OK then! I'm going.
    What? ... oh ... please don't go,
    Polly!

  d He won't show me those
    holiday photos, you know!
    Why won't he show you them?
    I don't know.

4 Emphatic stress

2 **T5.4**

Sally I'm going to meet Ann,
Grandfather.

Grandfather You're going to meet
Sam? Who's Sam?

Sally Not Sam – Ann. We're
going to play tennis.

Grandfather You're going to play
with Dennis? And who's
Dennis?

Sally Not Dennis. Tennis. We're
going to play tennis in the park.

Grandfather You're going to play
with Dennis and Mark? Who
are all these boys you're going
to meet?

Sally I'm not going to meet any
boys, Grandfather. I'm going
to play tennis – in the park –
with Ann, a girl ..., oh, never
mind ... see you later!

Grandfather Dennis ...? Mark ...?
Sam ...? The girl's going mad!

The words are all stressed to give
them special emphasis for some
reason:

• Because the speaker is
  surprised (for example when
  Grandfather says *Sam* or
  Dennis).

• Because the speaker wants to
  correct what the other person
  is saying (for example when
  Sally says *Not Sam – Ann*).

• Because the speaker is
  impatient (for example when
  Sally says *I'm not going to meet
  any boys*).

5 Stress and the sound /ə/ in word families

1

Verb	Adjective	Noun
arrange	—	arrangement
cancel	—	cancellation
—	cultural	culture
—	geographical	geography
—	historical	history
inform	informative	information
—	luxurious	luxury
—	popular	popularity
—	touristy	tourism

T5.5

arrangement ... arrange
cancel ... cancellation
cultural ... culture
geographical ... geography
history ... historical
inform ... information ...
  informative
luxury ... luxurious
popularity ... popular
tourism ... touristy

2

Verb	Adjective	Noun
arrange	—	arrangement
cancel	—	cancellation
—	cultural	culture
—	geographical	geography
—	historical	history
inform	informative	information
—	luxurious	luxury
—	popular	popularity
—	touristy	tourism

The stress pattern sometimes changes.

3

Verb	Adjective	Noun
arrange	—	arrangement
cancel	—	cancellation
—	cultural	culture
—	geographical	geography
—	historical	history
inform	informative	information
—	luxurious	luxury
—	popular	popularity
—	touristy	tourism

Unit 6

1 The sounds /n/ and /ŋ/

1   **T6.1a**
  a Look at those *fans*!
  b She *rang* up earlier.
  c Were you surprised by the *bang*?
  d I'd love a *win*.
  e How do you spell '*tongue*'?
  f This is *Ron*.

3 youngest
   language
   singer
   longer
   ingredients
   finger
   ringing
   banging
   young
   England

2 The sounds /ʊ/ and /u:/

2 a good food
   b a beautiful cooker
   c school uniform
   d a wooden pulley
   e Tuesday's newspapers
   f a souvenir bull
   g a cookery book
   h a menu for two

3 Showing degrees of enthusiasm

1 c ✳✳✳   e ✳✳✳
   d ✳   f ✳

4 Disappearing sounds and word linking

1 a 1 ✔   d 1 ✘
      2 ✔   2 ✔
      3 ✘   3 ✘
   b 1 ✔   e 1 ✘
      2 ✔   2 ✔
      3 ✘   3 ✘
   c 1 ✘
      2 ✔
      3 ✘

2 a consonant
   b vowel

5 International food words

2 a yoghurt /ˈjɒgət/
   b ketchup /ˈketʃʌp/
   c mayonnaise /ˌmeɪəˈneɪz/
   d hamburger /ˈhæmbɜ:gə/
   e chocolate /ˈtʃɒklət/
   f margarine /ˌmɑ:dʒəˈri:n/
   g champagne /ʃæmˈpeɪn/
   h tea /ti:/
   i oranges /ˈɒrɪndʒɪz/
   j pizza /ˈpi:tsə/
   k sandwich /ˈsænwɪdʒ/
   l mustard /ˈmʌstəd/
   m biscuits /ˈbɪskɪts/
   n bananas /bəˈnɑ:nəz/

Unit 7

1 The sounds /æ/ and /ʌ/

1 a ran ... run
   b sang ... sung
   c rang ... rung
   d swam ... swum
   e began ... begun
   f drank ... drunk

3   **T7.1b**
   a ran
   b sang
   c rung
   d swum
   e begun
   f drank

4 a drank
   b rang
   c has already begun
   d have just swum
   e drank
   f ran

5 a ✘   d ✘
   b ✔   e ✔
   c ✔   f ✘

2 The sound /h/

1 b Have you heard about Hanna's horrific adventure in Hamburg?
   c Henry's Uncle Herbert has had another heart attack in hospital.
   d Old Harry hasn't eaten his ham and eggs already, has he?
   e Hazel and Alan have had another unhappy holiday hitch-hiking in Austria and Hungary.

2 a has ... her
   c has
   d his ... he
   e have

Auxiliary verbs in their weak form (*has* / *have*), possessive adjectives (*his* / *her*), and the subject pronoun *he* in the middle of a sentence often have silent *h*. (The same thing also happens with the object pronouns *him* and *her*.)

Without the /h/ sound they can be said more quickly when they are in the middle of a sentence.

4 hour
vehicle
ghost
exhibition
dishonest
honest
heir

3 The weak forms of *for*

1 /fə/   /fər/
for ten years   for a week or two
for two minutes   for a long time
for five days   for a year
for six months   for ever

T7.3a

for ten years
for two minutes
for a week or two
for five days
for a long time
for a year
for ever
for six months

2 /fə/ is followed by a consonant; /fər/ is followed by a vowel.

We pronounce the /r/ to link it with the next word.

3 **T7.3b**

a How long have you known her?
Oh, I've known her for fourteen years.

b How long has she worked here?
Oh, she's worked here for ages and ages.

c How long have you had that car?
Oh, I've had it for a couple of months.

d How long has he been ill?
Oh, he's been ill for four or five days.

e How long have they been married?
Oh, they've been married for twenty-five years.

f How long have your parents gone away for?
Oh, they've gone away for a fortnight.

4 Question tags with falling intonation

1 **T7.4a**

Margaret You went to Manchester University, didn't you?
Steve Yes, that's right.
Margaret But you've worked in Canada for the last ten years, haven't you?
Steve Yes, I have.

2 Margaret already knows these facts about Steve. She is only asking to check her information.

4 **T7.4c**

a You studied computer science at university, didn't you?
b You finished your degree in 1987, didn't you?
c You've worked for Banana Computers since then, haven't you?
d You went to Canada in 1989, didn't you?
e You've also worked in Australia, haven't you?
f You lived in Melbourne, didn't you?

5 Stress in multi-word verbs

2 **T7.5a**

a Can you pick up the receiver, please?
Can you pick the receiver up, please?
b Look up the new words in your dictionaries.
Look the new words up in your dictionaries.
c We had to put off the meeting because of the terrible weather.
We had to put the meeting off because of the terrible weather.
d At bedtime my mother used to make up wonderful stories for us.
At bedtime my mother used to make wonderful stories up for us.
e His parents brought up James and his brothers very strictly.
His parents brought James and his brothers up very strictly.

When multi-word verbs are separated, the preposition is stressed.

When multi-word verbs are not separated, the preposition is not stressed.

3 **T7.5c**

a I think Emma's gone out with her boyfriend somewhere tonight.
b Do you get on with your mother-in-law OK?
c We're really looking forward to your party – it'll be great to see you!
d We've run out of nice bread – could you get some more when you go to the shops?
e Unfortunately he fell out with his parents last year for some reason – they haven't spoken to each other since then, apparently!

4 b

Unit 8

1 The sounds /ɔ:/ and /əʊ/

1 a 1   b 2   c 2   d 1   e 2

T8.1c

a What a big hall!
b Can I have that bowl?
c Shall I sew that for you?
d I like that boar!
e What a lot of notes!

2 /ɔ:/   /əʊ/
law   no
four   home
causes   broken
door   oldest
organization   go
horse   won't

2 The sounds /b/ and /v/

1 **T8.2c**

a Would you like a *vet*?
b I only want the *best*.
c Shall we take a *boat*?
d Hmm, there's something wrong with your *vowels*.
e There are some *bats* in the cellar.

3 Intonation with *really* and *absolutely*

2
● hilarious ● delicious ● fascinating
● terrified ● exhausted ● filthy

2 **T8.3b**

a **A** Are you tired?
  B I'm absolutely exhausted.
b **A** Was the kitchen a bit dirty?
  B It was really filthy.
c **A** Are those sausages tasty?
  B They're absolutely delicious.
d **A** Was that film funny?
  B It was really hilarious.
e **A** That book seems interesting.
  B It's absolutely fascinating.
f **A** Were you frightened by the ghost?
  B We were really terrified.

4 Contractions of *will* and *would*

2 a *1* 'll go ... stops
  b *2* 'd help ... asked
  c *2* 'd work ... paid
  d *1* 'll be ... tell
  e *2* stopped ... 'd get
  f *1* 's ... 'll stay

T8.4a

a Are you going jogging?
  I'll go if it stops raining.
b I think she needs help.
  Well, I'd help her if she asked me.
c Can't you work a bit faster?
  I'd work faster if you paid me more.
d What's the matter?
  You'll be angry if I tell you ...
e He's got a terrible cough.
  Yes. If he stopped smoking, it'd get better.
f Are you going clubbing this evening?
  If there's a football match on TV, I'll stay at home.

5 Adjectives ending in *-ed* and *-ing*

1 **T8.5b**

a She's always very *tired*.
b Your uncle was *fascinating*.
c I felt very *bored* at the party.

d Your granny's a very *frightening* woman.
e I'm looking for a boyfriend. Is your brother *interested*?
f Your aunt was *amazing* when I told her we were getting married.

2 a She's always very tired.
  6 Yes. She doesn't get enough sleep.

b Your uncle was fascinating.
  4 Yes. He's a wonderful person.

c I felt very bored at the party.
  5 Wasn't there anyone to talk to then?

d Your granny's a very frightening woman.
  3 Yes. As children, we felt really afraid of her.

e I'm looking for a boyfriend. Is your brother interested?
  1 I'm not sure. I know he likes you a lot.

f Your aunt was amazing when I told her we were getting married.
  2 Yes. She offered to organize the whole wedding – flowers, food, clothes, honeymoon, everything.

Unit 9

1 The sound /ɜː/

1 All the underlined vowel sounds are spelt differently, but they are all pronounced /ɜː/.

2 a ti<u>r</u>ed /aɪə/   d b<u>u</u>ry /e/
  b w<u>o</u>rn /ɔː/   e w<u>ea</u>r /eə/
  c west<u>e</u>rn /ə/

3 **A** Are all your friends from university w<u>o</u>rking now?
  B Nearly. K<u>i</u>rsty's doing res<u>ea</u>rch w<u>o</u>rk at B<u>i</u>rmingham University and Sh<u>i</u>rley's gone to w<u>o</u>rk as a n<u>u</u>rse somewhere in B<u>u</u>rma.
  A Really? That's adventurous. What about P<u>ea</u>rl?
  B Oh, P<u>ea</u>rl's a civil s<u>e</u>rvant now. She and K<u>i</u>rk live in a sub<u>u</u>rb somewhere.

A And how about D<u>i</u>rk?
B Oh, haven't you h<u>ea</u>rd about D<u>i</u>rk? He's w<u>o</u>rking in T<u>u</u>rkey as a winds<u>u</u>rf instructor! He's l<u>ea</u>rnt T<u>u</u>rkish and he's <u>ea</u>rning a fortune ... or so I've h<u>ea</u>rd.

2 Weak forms with present and past modals

2 a *E* b *E* c *B* d *A* e *A* f *B*

T9.2a

a It must be hard to believe what's happened!
b It must have been a big shock for her family!
c She might never have found the lottery ticket!
d The baby can't have been very big!
e It could have been dangerous for her and the baby.
f She might be changing her mind about going to university now she's rich!

3 Sentence stress with *So do I*, etc.

1 ✔ South London   ✔ Croydon
  ✗ camping   ✗ sightseeing
  ✔ the price of accommodation in the city centre
  ✗ how long they've been on holiday

T9.3a

Zoe Hi, I just heard you talking to the waiter. You're English, aren't you?
Rob Yeah, I'm from South London, actually.
Zoe Really, so am I ... whereabouts?
Rob Well, it's Croydon to be exact.
Zoe Yeah? Me too! Which part of Croydon ...

Zoe So where are you staying?
Rob Santa Marina, just down the coast – we can't afford the city centre, unfortunately.
Zoe No, neither can we ... it's lovely though, isn't it?
Rob Yeah, beautiful ... but really expensive, but it's much cheaper in Santa Marina – we're staying in a bed and breakfast.

Zoe Oh, we aren't – we're camping. It's really good fun.

Rob Really? What's the campsite like ...

Rob So are you having a good time?

Zoe Yeah, but we've only been here for three days, and so far we've spent nearly all our time on the beach – we haven't done much sightseeing.

Rob Oh, we have, we've been here about ten days and we've travelled ...

2 `T9.3c`

a I haven't got any money with me.
  Don't worry, I have.

b My English teacher comes from Australia.
  Really? So does mine!

c I hate all this traffic and pollution!
  Yes, so do I.

d In our class we get homework every night.
  Really? We don't.

e I can't understand this exercise at all!
  Neither can I!

4 Adjectives ending in -al, -ful, -able / -ible, and -ous

1 b miserable   d delicious
  c generous   e hilarious

2 `T9.4a`

ending in -al	ending in -able / -ible
commercial	miserable
financial	sociable
practical	sensible
	terrible

ending in -ful	ending in -ous
careful	generous
cheerful	delicious
wonderful	marvellous
awful	hilarious

3 `T9.4b`

a dangerous   e ambitious
b theoretical   f useful
c international   g religious
d courageous   h furious

Unit 10

1 The sounds /e/ and /eɪ/

1 a 2 ... 1   d 2 ... 1
  b 2 ... 1   e 1 ... 2
  c 1 ... 2   f 1 ... 2

`T10.1a`

a laid ... led   d saint ... scent
b bait ... bet   e men ... mane
c test ... taste   f cell ... sale

2 a 1   f 2
  b 2   g 1
  c 1   h 2
  d 1   i 1
  e 2   j 2

2 The sounds /r/ and /l/

2 a is pronounced
  b is not pronounced

3 `T10.2b`

a That's a nice *lake*.
b They *grow* at night.
c Have you seen my *parrot*?
d She's finished her book about *glamour*.
e He *collected* the homework.

3 Correcting politely with the Present Perfect Continuous

1 a **A** So you've been collecting coins for 10 years ...
   B Well, no, actually. I've been collecting stamps for 10 years.

b **A** So you've been smoking since you were 16 ...
   B Well, no, actually. I've been smoking since I was 11.

c **A** So you've been driving for 6 years ...
   B Well, no, actually. I've been driving for 6 months.

d **A** So you've been drinking my beer by mistake ...
   B Well, no, actually. Pete's been drinking your beer by mistake.

e **A** So you've been writing poems for 20 years ...
   B Well, no, actually. I've been writing poems for 30 years.

f **A** So you've been relaxing in Prague since April ...
   B Well, no, actually. I've been working in Prague since April.

2 `T10.3b`

a So you've been living in Rome for 10 years.
  Well, no actually. I've been living in Paris for 10 years.

b So you've been playing golf for five years.
  Well, no, actually. I've been playing tennis for five years.

c So you've been decorating the house since Monday ...
  Well, no, actually. I've been decorating the house since Friday.

d So you've been doing the gardening since lunchtime ...
  Well, no, actually. I've been doing the housework since lunchtime.

e So you've been washing the car this morning.
  Well, no, actually. I've been repairing the car this morning.

f So you've been revising for exams all day ...
  Well, no, actually. I've been revising for exams all week.

4 Strong and weak forms of prepositions

2 `T10.4b`

a **A** How long are you here for?
   B Only for another week at the most.

b **C** What did her mother die of?
   D I'm not sure. Of cancer, I think.

c **E** But where did you get the idea from?
   F From my time as a tourist in India, actually.
   E And which publisher did you go to?
   F To Camford University Press, of course.

3 a **A** S
  B W ... W
 b **C** S
  D W
 c **E** S
  F W ... W
  E S
  F W ... W

The strong forms are used when the prepositions are at the end of the sentence.

5 Stress in compound nouns

1 **T10.5**

a washing | fax | machine
  sewing

b phone | box
  card
  book

c arm | wheel | chair
  push

d nail | brush
  file
  varnish

e wine | roof | rack
  luggage

f key | board
  hole
  ring

2 The first word carries the main stress in each case. This the usual stress pattern in compounds formed with noun + noun.

Unit 11

1 The sounds /ʃ/ and /tʃ/

1 a sherry   d witch
  b chin   e chops
  c ships   f wash

T11.1a

a sherry ... cherry ... sherry
b shin ... chin ... chin
c ships ... ships ... chips
d wish ... witch ... witch
e shops ... chops ... chops
f wash ... wash ... watch

4 <u>Ch</u>ristmas /k/   Ru<u>ssi</u>an /ʃ/
  explana<u>ti</u>on /ʃ/   ma<u>ch</u>ine /ʃ/

Other examples of these exceptions:

- *ch* = /k/ in *Christian, chemist's, chaos* (words of Greek origin)
- *ti* = /ʃ/ in *pollution, generation, dictionary* (words of Latin origin)
- *ssi* = /ʃ/ in *expression, impression, passion* (words of Latin origin)
- *ch* = /ʃ/ in *chauffeur, chef, champagne* (words of French origin)

7 a Which of <u>Sh</u>irley Hat<u>ch</u>ard's <u>ch</u>ildren stole a por<u>ti</u>on of <u>ch</u>erry <u>ch</u>eesecake from the kit<u>ch</u>en <u>sh</u>elf?

b <u>Sh</u>eila <u>Ch</u>arlton's <u>Cz</u>ech wa<u>sh</u>ing ma<u>ch</u>ine <u>ch</u>ewed up Ri<u>ch</u>ard <u>Sh</u>eridan's <u>ch</u>ecked <u>sh</u>orts.

c The ri<u>ch</u> Turki<u>sh</u> <u>sug</u>ar mer<u>ch</u>ant pur<u>ch</u>ased a <u>sh</u>ining Por<u>sch</u>e for his <u>Ch</u>inese <u>ch</u>auffeur to poli<u>sh</u>.

d Sa<u>sh</u>a, the Ru<u>ss</u>ian <u>ch</u>ess <u>ch</u>ampion, <u>ch</u>ased <u>Sh</u>aron, the Scotti<u>sh</u> <u>ch</u>ambermaid, round the kit<u>ch</u>en, so <u>Sh</u>aron <u>sh</u>owed Sa<u>sh</u>a the door.

2 The sound /aʊ/

1 a f<u>our</u> /ɔ:/   d r<u>ou</u>te /u:/
  b l<u>ow</u>er /əʊ/   e gr<u>ow</u>n /əʊ/
  c sh<u>ow</u> /əʊ/

2 **T11.2b**

a I found £50 lying on the ground when I was in town this morning.

b Laura's going to show you round the house now.

c We caught a little brown mouse in the shower room downstairs this morning.

d They've got a town house and a country house, you know.

e They lowered the cow from the window of the tower to the ground.

3 Understanding fast speech

4 **T11.3**

a Could you tell me what time it is, please?
(9 words)

b Excuse me, do you know if there's a post office near here?
(13 words)

c Can you tell me if there's a phone in here, please?
(12 words)

d Have you any idea if there's a cash machine nearby, please?
(12 words)

e Excuse me, do you know how far it is to the nearest station?
(13 words)

f Excuse me, have you any idea what time this place closes?
(11 words)

4 Rising and falling intonation in question tags

3 a U   d S
  b S   e U
  c S

T11.4b

a They don't drive on the left in Australia, do they?

b They speak Portuguese in Brazil, don't they?

c St Petersburg used to be called Leningrad, didn't it?

d Austria hasn't got a king or queen, has it?

e Scotland's got its own national football team, hasn't it?

4 The correct information is:

c Amsterdam is the capital of the Netherlands.

d They've got a king in Spain.

e The Russian Revolution was in 1917.

f Oregon's on the west coast of America.

g The moon isn't as big as the Earth.

h New York is bigger than Los Angeles (in terms of population).

i Greenland isn't an independent country – it's a Danish territory.

j Seeing a black cat is good luck, according to English superstition.

5 Transcribing words about city life

1 `T11.5a`
a It's usually very crowded.
b It can be very noisy.
c There's often lots of nightlife.
d It can be lonely.
e There's often a lot of crime.
f There's not much green space.
g There's often a lot of pollution.
h It's often very lively.
i There are lots of restaurants, shops, and theatres.
j It's usually busy.
k There's lots of variety.
l It's not very peaceful.

3 a nightlife (lively, lots of variety)
b pollution (crowded)
c not much green space

`T11.5b`
a There are dozens of pubs and clubs – you can stay out all night if you want to!
b The worst thing is, it's just so filthy from all the cars ... the smoke's terrible ... you feel as if you can't breathe sometimes.
c One thing I miss are all the parks there were in the city where I grew up ... there are hardly any parks here.

Unit 12

1 Vowel and diphthong sounds

1 `T12.1a`
a working /ɜː/   d part /ɑː/
b week /iː/   e talk /ɔː/
c moon /uː/

2 `T12.1b`
a son /ʌ/   e good /ʊ/
b police /ə/   f business /ɪ/
c dog /ɒ/   g rest /e/
d black /æ/

3 `T12.1c`
a /ʊə/ tour
b /eɪ/ aw<u>ay</u>
c /ɔɪ/ enj<u>oy</u>
d /aɪ/ sky
e /aʊ/ now
f /əʊ/ teleph<u>o</u>ne
g /ɪə/ here
h /eə/ wear

2 Consonant sounds

1 `T12.2a`
a /p/ <u>p</u>oor   f /θ/ <u>th</u>ink
b /t/ <u>t</u>ea   g /s/ <u>c</u>inema
c /k/ <u>c</u>alm   h /ʃ/ <u>s</u>ure
d /tʃ/ <u>ch</u>ild   i /h/ <u>h</u>ouse
e /f/ <u>ph</u>oto

2 `T12.2b`
a /b/ <u>b</u>oy   i /m/ <u>m</u>an
b /d/ <u>d</u>oor   j /n/ <u>n</u>ose
c /g/ <u>g</u>ood   k /ŋ/ ri<u>ng</u>
d /dʒ/ <u>s</u>trange l /l/ <u>l</u>ight
e /v/ <u>v</u>isitor   m /r/ <u>fr</u>iend
f /ð/ <u>m</u>other   n /w/ <u>w</u>ell
g /z/ clo<u>s</u>ed   o /j/ <u>y</u>oung
h /ʒ/ plea<u>s</u>ure

3 Showing disbelief

1 Speaker **B** doesn't believe what Elaine said. On the word *said*, she uses special stress and her intonation goes down.

2 c ✘   e ✘

4 Contractions, linking, and weak forms

1 `T12.4a`
a I don't like funerals.
b I've been to three christenings this year.
c She isn't married.
d He's wearing one striped sock and one checked sock.
e I can't wait!
f They're eating sandwiches.

3 a ✘   e ✘
  b ✔   f ✘
  c ✘   g ✔
  d ✔

d Fin<u>d it</u> in the picture.
g I can'<u>t</u> understand.

4 The underlined words are all weak forms.

5 Words with silent letters

1 b ~~w~~reath
  c bouq~~uet~~
  d ~~k~~nock~~ed~~
  e marri~~a~~ge
  f g~~u~~idance
  g nei~~gh~~bou~~rs~~
  h ex~~h~~austed

2 a ✔   e ✘
  b ✘   f ✘
  c ✘   g ✔
  d ✔   h ✔

Oxford University Press
Great Clarendon Street, Oxford OX2 6DP

Oxford   New York
Athens   Auckland   Bangkok   Bogotá
Buenos Aires   Calcutta   Cape Town   Chennai
Dar es Salaam   Delhi   Florence   Hong Kong
Istanbul   Karachi   Kuala Lumpur   Madrid
Melbourne   Mexico City   Mumbai   Nairobi
Paris   São Paulo   Singapore   Taipei   Tokyo
Toronto   Warsaw

and associated companies in
Berlin   Ibadan

OXFORD and OXFORD ENGLISH are trade marks of
Oxford University Press

ISBN 0 19 436245 0

© Oxford University Press 1999

Acknowledgements

The authors would like to acknowledge their debt to
the writers of various standard pronunciation reference
books, especially:
Ann Baker *Introducing English Pronunciation*
A.C.Gimson *A Practical Course of English Pronunciation*
Joanne Kenworthy *Teaching English Pronunciation*
Colin Mortimer *Elements of Pronunciation*
P.Roach *English Phonetics and Phonology*

Illustrations by:
Kathy Baxendale (33)
Brett Breckon (29, 45)
James Griffiths (11, 15, 23, 30, 35)
Joanna Kerr (17)
Nigel Paige (8, 10, 11, 16, 18, 19, 20, 21, 22, 23, 24, 25, 26,
   27, 30, 31, 33, 34, 35, 37, 38, 42, 43, 46, 47, 48, 52, 53)
Kath Walker (13)

**The publisher would like to thank the following
for their permission to reproduce photographs:**
Art Directors & TRIP Photo Library (39)
Camera Press Ltd (15 Bardot, Tung)
The Image Bank (40)
Popperfoto (15 Blair, Redford)
Frank Spooner Pictures Ltd (15 Goldberg)

Commissioned photography by:
Paul Freestone

Freelance art editor:
Mandy Twells

Design by:
Holdsworth Associates, Isle of Wight

Cover design by:
Rowie Christopher

The authors and publisher are grateful to those who
have given permission to reproduce the following
extracts and adaptations of copyright material:
'Celebration' by Willis Hall, reproduced by permission
of Alexandra Cann Representation.